Teaching English

Teaching Young Language Learners Through Stories

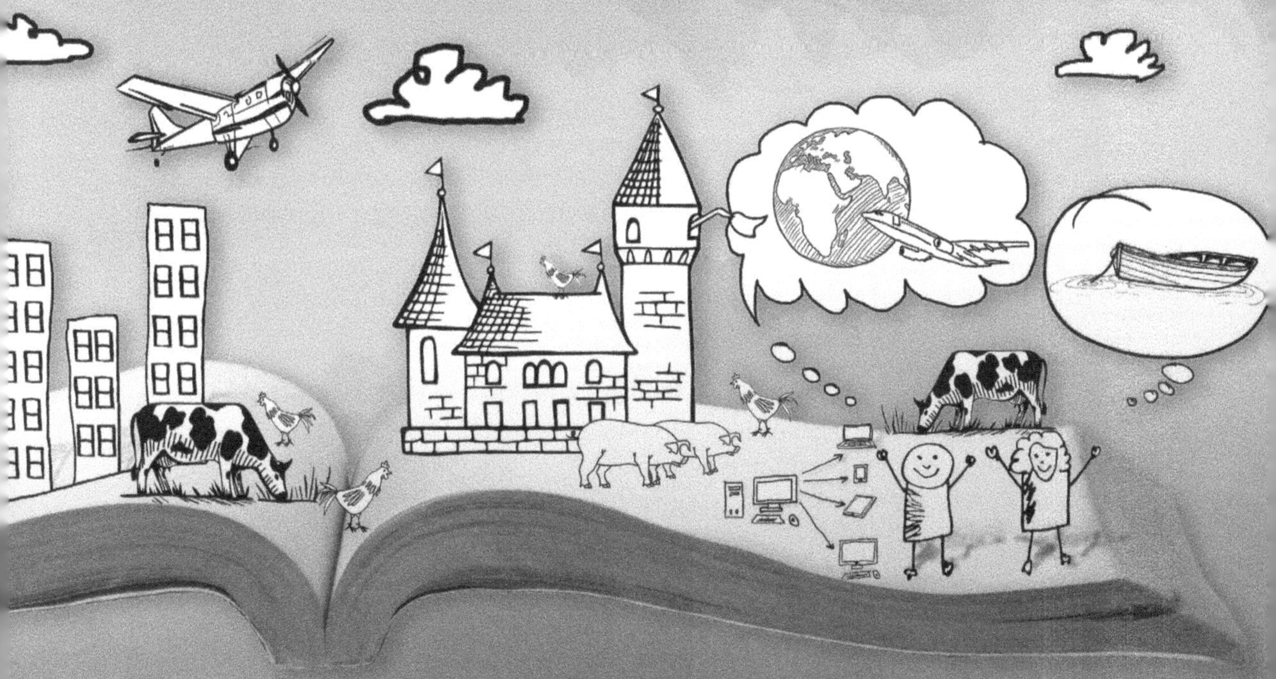

Using stories and children's fiction to motivate your primary learners and improve learning outcomes

Sharon Ahlquist

Teaching Young Language Learners Through Stories:

Using stories and children's fiction to motivate your primary learners and improve learning outcomes

Published by:
Pavilion Publishing and Media Ltd
Blue Sky Offices
25 Cecil Pashley Way
Shoreham by Sea, West Sussex
BN43 5FF

Tel: 01273 434 943
Email: info@pavpub.com
Web: www.pavpub.com

Published 2024

A catalogue record for this book is available from the British Library.

ISBN: 978-1-80388-340-3

Pavilion Publishing and Media is a leading publisher of books, training materials and digital content in mental health, social care and allied fields. Pavilion and its imprints offer must-have knowledge and innovative learning solutions underpinned by sound research and professional values.

Author: Sharon Ahlquist
Editor: Penny Hands/Mike Benge
Cover design: Emma Dawe, Pavilion Publishing and Media Ltd
Page layout and typesetting: Emma Dawe, Pavilion Publishing and Media Ltd
Printing: Independent Publishers Group (IPG)

Contents

Introduction

'Exciting, funny, fun – I'd like to have it again!' These were the words of a Swedish 11-year-old on finishing four weeks of English lessons based on Roald Dahl's *The Magic Finger* (Puffin, 2016). During this time, the children had worked in groups and pairs, as well as on their own, listening to their teacher reading to them, and reading quietly to themselves. They had worked with a variety of tasks based on the text. These included sequencing, matching, predicting (for example, drawing a picture of what might happen next), crosswords and bingo. Their enthusiasm would gladden the heart of any teacher. So, what is it that makes stories and children's fiction suitable for young language learners?

First, let's consider what we mean by young learners, and which language we are referring to. For the purposes of this book, young learners are considered to be children aged between 6 and 13, and the language can be any language, including the learner's first language. While my main focus is the 6-13 age range, I also consider older learners and adults in each chapter. Much of the work described is based on my own experience as a researcher and teacher educator in Sweden, where I train teachers to teach English in primary and secondary school – in other words, English as a foreign language. However, the classroom activities described in this book will be appropriate for teachers who teach other foreign languages, and for those who are working in first-language contexts. In the United Kingdom, for instance, this might include English-speaking children learning French or Spanish, as well as those for whom English is an additional language to the one they speak at home. By virtue of their young age, all primary-age children are language learners because they are still learning the language of the world around them. This book is therefore also intended to be useful to primary teachers teaching the first language.

Characteristics of young language learners

Over the last few years, there has been a considerable increase in the amount of research carried out with this age group. As more children worldwide begin their formal education in English at an early age, so research interest has grown. One thing we know is that they enjoy tasks which let them use their imagination. Any classroom teacher can tell you that children have vivid imaginations, which they reveal when they write stories, create and act out role plays or speculate about what might happen next in a chain of events. I have seen this in my own research with children (Ahlquist, 2013; 2020). They also learn implicitly, picking up words and phrases as they encounter them. Then, at around the age of 11, they start to analyse the language they encounter, and teachers might find they ask them things like 'Why is it one dog: two dogs, but one sheep: two sheep?'

They also like to work in collaboration with others, in pairs or in groups. One reason for this is that it is fun, but they also benefit from being able to learn from and help each other. This is what Pinter (2007) found when she studied two 10-year-old Hungarian boys working on spot-the-difference tasks. She found that they enjoyed the challenge of using their joint language resources to solve a puzzle together. A key word here is 'challenge', which I will come back to at the end of this section. In Pinter's study, neither boy had worked on this kind of task before, and they described it as quite tricky, observing, however, that things are easier when you are relaxed.

From a sociocultural perspective, learning is said to occur when a learner works together with a more able other, and it is during such times that learning becomes visible (Vygotsky, 1978). In practical terms, this can be problematic. If the proficiency levels are too different, the less able learner may not benefit from the partner's help, and the more able partner may be frustrated both with a task that is too easy and the fact of having to support a peer, especially if this is regular classroom practice. Vygotsky's theory is also based on the assumption that the learners are willing to give and receive help; as such, the learners' personal relationship is also a factor in successful collaboration. In Pinter's study, the two boys were friends, working on something that was a novelty for them, and they were both challenged by it. Even though one was more proficient in English than the other, there were occasions when the less proficient partner was able to supply a word that was needed.

Other studies have looked at how young learners' characteristics change over time. Researchers in the Early Language Learning in Europe (ELLiE) study tracked the second language development of 1,400 children in seven European countries from the ages of 6 to 10 (Enever, 2011). They found that the learners continued to enjoy pair work and group work, but that as they got older, they tended to consider the games and songs that had characterised their lessons in the early years (and which they had enjoyed) as childish. They saw the introduction of a coursebook as a signal that the more serious work was now beginning, and they looked forward to the change.

However, teachers often find that children's initial enthusiasm for the coursebook soon fades if it is the main or only source of classroom work. There is also a tendency for motivation to decrease as children get older (Enever, 2011). Overuse of a coursebook might account for this loss of interest up to a point, but there is more to it. For example, older learners experience biological and emotional changes as they approach puberty. It is a time when they are starting to form a self-image, which is influenced by how their peers see them. Many aspects of life can be embarrassing, and this includes having to speak another language in front of others. The learner has two chances to get things wrong: a factual answer and a mispronunciation or incorrect formulation of a sentence, with the added possibility of public correction by the teacher. The phenomenon of language anxiety (for example, Horwitz, 2010) is one that many teachers and student teachers recognise from their own school days. Language anxiety means being afraid of speaking in front of others. There can be a variety of reasons for this – perhaps the learner is shy, and reluctant to speak even in their first language. It can also be that previously someone has laughed at them; they remember the experience, and it has a negative effect on their attitude to using the language.

Researchers in the field argue that learning is influenced by emotions: we learn with our heads and our hearts. More than forty years ago, Krashen (1982) used the metaphor of the 'affective filter' to describe what happens in a learning context. When a learner is engaged and relaxed, as the boys in Pinter's study were, the filter is low and they learn. On the other hand, when the learner is anxious, tired or bored, the filter is high and this blocks learning.

Returning to the notion of 'challenge', another aspect of Krashen's theory regarding second language learning is the 'comprehensible input hypothesis'. Krashen argues that for learning to take place, the level of the reading material should be just beyond the current ability of the learner. He stresses that input not only needs to be understandable, but compelling (Krashen & Bland, 2014). In reviewing the applicability of Krashen's views forty years on, Lichten and Vanpatten (2021) highlight the importance of classroom activities in which the learner engages with the input and can show that they have understood it. So, let us go on then to consider where stories come into this.

Coursebooks

Coursebooks remain the predominant type of teaching material throughout the world (Gray, 2016). Basing lessons on a coursebook has its advantages. Firstly, many learners like them: they provide a clear structure; each chapter has a topic with a core vocabulary and grammar focus; workbook exercises allow learners to practise the new language. Not least, the coursebook provides a record of what has been covered, all in the one book, making it easy to look back.

For the busy or inexperienced teacher, a coursebook is reassuring; it has been designed with a syllabus in mind. If produced for the international market, it may be based on the Common European Framework (CEFR) scales. If produced domestically, it will be more explicitly related to the requirements of the national curriculum, though that in itself may be based on the CEFR scales, as is often the case in western Europe. Alternatively, the book may have to be approved by a government department for education in accordance with strict guidelines. In other words, if teachers follow the coursebook, they know that the children will cover what they are supposed to cover. This is important where coursebook content is closely tied to national tests. Teacher's notes provide guidance on how to work with the coursebook content, and there are often supplementary materials in the form of digital links, or books that focus specifically on building vocabulary.

While it is true that coursebooks can soon become out of date and may be expensive to replace, the problems really start when the coursebook is the only source of lesson content. The routine of following the same chapter layout and task-type week after week may appeal to some, but for other learners the predictability becomes monotonous. Further, certain exercises and reading texts may be difficult for less proficient learners, while failing to challenge the more proficient ones.

Stories in coursebooks offer some variation. One problem with these, though, is that they are often written to illustrate a new grammatical structure and are not necessarily engaging. In addition, due to space limitations, coursebook stories tend to be quite short. As such, they offer little challenge for the more proficient and deny all readers an opportunity to get into the world of the story and enjoy reading about the characters in it.

One supposed benefit of working with a coursebook is that vocabulary introduced in one chapter is then recycled in the next, and that different kinds of task, whether in the coursebook or workbook, consciously include the new vocabulary and thus facilitate learning. This supports reading development because learners need to know at least 95% of words to understand what they are reading (Laufer & Aviad-Levitzky, 2017). However, surveys of the coursebooks used in upper primary in Sweden (Nordlund, 2016) have found an absence of such strategies. Nordlund and Norberg (2020) refer to research conducted on coursebooks used in both Spain and Japan which produced similar findings. Researchers in this field argue that new words should be met again soon after the first encounter, and in different contexts, so that networks can be formed in the learner's brain. However, the learner needs to notice the words in the first place (Schmidt, 2010). If a learner is sufficiently interested in what they are reading – if they are absorbed in a story, for example – they may notice words, think about what they mean and remember them. So, let us look at how stories not only help to develop vocabulary and reading skills but can also be used to address the wider syllabus for English.

Stories and children's fiction

Challenges and benefits of using authentic texts in the language classroom

An alternative to using the coursebook alone is to base lessons on stories or on works of fiction. There are challenges in choosing an authentic text, i.e. a text in which the target language is genuine and 'not originally intended for language learning or teaching' (Long, 2020). An 11-year-old learner with limited exposure to the second language may struggle with a book written for a first-language learner of the same age. Yet if they are presented with a book that is linguistically simpler, the topic might seem too childish for them. However, challenging young learners to read authentic stories above their language level can be successful due to what is termed the 'Harry Potter effect'. This was first noticed some years ago when children could not wait for the translation of the latest Harry Potter book, so they would dive straight into it in English. This highlights the importance of motivation, which is known to have a positive effect on learning (Lamb, 2017). While not every book can have the Harry Potter effect, it shows that learners are able to enjoy what they are reading even though they do not understand every word. In these conditions, they are developing the useful life skill of accepting uncertainty and making a best guess at meaning in context. To do this, they are using both linguistic knowledge and knowledge of the fictional world.

The power of the image

There is a broad range of fiction available today, even for the youngest readers, starting with richly illustrated and appealing picturebooks. The power of visual imagery in supporting learning has been the focus of much research. Kaminski (2013), for instance, has reported on how working with images before reading a text can help the learners understand what they read. In the digital age, stories and books can be encountered through visual resources such as video clips and games, which support understanding and have the potential to deepen the learner's understanding of the story. Brunsmeier and Kolb (2017) have found that story apps can provide an opportunity for interaction with the text, and that this enhances opportunities for learning. Interaction can take many forms, such as completing a task or puzzle.

Teaching values through stories

The second reason for teaching through stories is the opportunity they offer to consider fundamental values and ethics as part of the wider curriculum. In my study on *The Magic Finger*, referred to earlier, the children stated the following as examples of aspects of the book that they liked: *I like when she* (an insensitive teacher) *turned into a cat; I like when the ducks shot at the Gregg family*. (The family had been shooting at the ducks and now got a taste of their own medicine.) There was a belief among the children, or most of them, that hunting animals for fun is wrong; they appreciated what they saw as a happy, fair ending for all when the Greggs were finally returned to human form, reformed by their experience, and now animal lovers (Ahlquist, 2020). Most children expected a morally satisfying ending. However, I overheard two 10-year-old girls discussing what they thought would happen. One of them was sure it would be happy because 'all books have a happy ending'. The other was not so sure: 'But this is an English book', she said, doubtfully.

Working with cultural content

The remark above takes us on to another aspect of working with fiction. Second language syllabuses often state that young learners should read stories and that their exposure to different literary genres should increase as they get older. Exploring literature is also a way of working with the cultural content of a language syllabus, which begins in the younger years with learning about daily life and customs. Bland (2015) makes the point that working with fiction trains a learner's thinking skills – that they draw on an in-built framework of what can be expected. This might be challenged through encounters with other cultural norms and values, or not. That the young girl in my study even thought to question that there could be any other ending because it was an English (and not a Swedish) book shows an early awareness of this aspect of fiction. Through their reading, learners acquire knowledge not only about other cultures but also about other cultures in relation to their own. The aim here is to develop intercultural competence, a common component of a second language syllabus, in which learners are supposed to acquire knowledge, skills and attitudes in order to be able to interact effectively with those from different cultural backgrounds.

Skills development

Just as we can aim to develop our learners' intercultural competence through working with fiction in our language lessons, so we can use it as a basis for tasks which will promote the development of skills. The United Nations (UN) and the Organization for Economic Cooperation and Development (OECD) have identified certain skills as important for the 21st century, examples of which are: critical thinking, creativity, collaboration, communication and social skills. Teachers choose texts and design tasks to serve the dual purpose of developing linguistic and life skills such as the ability to work with others. Another topic for working with fiction might be the United Nations goals for sustainability, examples of which are climate and environmental issues, health, equality, and responsible consumption. The potential for working across the curriculum and from different perspectives is significant when we work with children's stories and fiction.

Linguistic knowledge

How can texts of this kind promote linguistic development? Ghosn (2013) maintains that when children read, they form mental images which help them to remember words. Where there are pictures, the link between words and meaning is reinforced. Cameron (2001) makes the point that words are automatically recycled in books, which is significant since, as we have seen, frequency is a factor in vocabulary acquisition. The words used to describe people, settings or situations in a work of fiction are likely to reappear throughout the book, providing the reader with opportunities to encounter them in a meaningful context. Pinter (2017) makes a similar point about the role that reading can play in developing knowledge of grammatical structure (such as the use of the past tense for narrative). Younger children learn implicitly, not by drawing on rules, and so when they encounter chunks of language in context, conditions are created for learning beyond the level of individual words.

Focus on form

Cameron (2001) argues that when children listen, their focus is on making sense of the story, and this is natural and desirable. But if the children are focusing on meaning, they cannot simultaneously focus on words or grammatical structures. If teachers want to develop their learners' knowledge of vocabulary and grammar, they need to create tasks which direct learners' attention to the language. Cameron defines 'task', or what the learners do with the language, as an 'environment for learning' (2001:21). In other words, when you design tasks, you are creating opportunities for your learners to learn. However, you can also limit the opportunities that individual learners have since you decide who does what and who gets to speak. One way to create learning opportunities, as Watkins (2018) suggests, is to involve the children in the telling of a story. The teacher does not just read the story to the class but, through asking questions about what has happened, or could happen, draws both on the children's cognitive framework of what can be expected and their linguistic resources.

In short, then, there are many arguments for working with fiction in the language classroom. Not only can we bring the world of the imagination as well as the wider world to our learners, but we can also integrate or adapt for our purposes the kinds of tasks (jigsaw or matching, for example) they know and enjoy. As Nikolov and Timpe-Laughlin (2021) have found, there is a correlation between learners' familiarity with a task and their level of achievement on that task, but enjoyment has a still greater effect. This is not something which surprises classroom teachers, but it is worth keeping in mind as we start to look at different kinds of fiction, and tasks which are designed to promote understanding, enjoyment and language development.

Guide to chapters

Chapter 1 considers how picturebooks and illustrated books can be used with different age groups. Chapter 2 introduces graphic novels, before moving on to Chapter 3, which considers graded readers (books written for specific language levels) and their place in the classroom. Chapter 4 looks at ways in which teachers can use fairy tales in their teaching with both younger and older learners. Chapter 5 proposes a number of ways in which novels and short stories can be best used in the classroom, and ways in which they can be exploited to teach reading skills and as vehicles for language development. Once the main story tools have been covered. Finally, Chapter 6 looks at how teachers can usefully use the Storyline approach with all kinds of fiction.

At the end of each chapter, you will find a section to help you with your continuing professional development. This is intended to help you to reflect on what you have just read and to consider how the ideas and activities discussed might work in your context. The tasks are there as prompts for experiential learning but can also be used as discussion points in any teacher development or teacher training session. At the end of each chapter, you will find suggestions for further reading. Full references for this book can be found in the Bibliography.

Professional development

Questions for reflection

- How important is it for you to use stories in class? Have you used them much in your teaching before getting this book? Why/Why not?
- Choose a story that you think would appeal to your class. Now consider the young learner characteristics outlined in the chapter and link them to the story and how you might work with it.

Things to try

- Look at your syllabus for English. Based on the story you chose above, create a task to work with one specific part of the syllabus

Further reading

Ghosn, I. K. (2013). *Storybridge to second language literacy: The theory, research and practice of teaching English with children's literature*. Charlotte, N.C: Information Age Publishing.

1. Picturebooks and illustrated books

What is the difference between an illustrated book and a picturebook? Although it is sometimes hard to make a distinction, the answer lies in the relationship between text and image. In an illustrated book, the text is the most important element (and was probably written first). The pictures show the reader what is stated in the text, often adding visual details which are not described. The pictures show the reader what people and places look like, as well as depicting events described in the text. An example of this kind is the work of Roald Dahl, which has been richly illustrated by Quentin Blake. In a picturebook, images are as important as the text in the telling of the story; the effect on the reader is dependent on the interaction between the two. There are also picturebooks with no text at all. An example of a wordless picturebook is Raymond Briggs' (1978) *The Snowman*, the story of a young boy who makes a snowman which comes to life in the night. The warmth of the relationship between two characters from different worlds and the excitement of their adventure is conveyed in the detail of the pictures.

Picturebooks as a source of language

Books without text

Even a book with no written words can be a rich source of language. When a parent or teacher tells a child a story and talks to them about it while pointing to the pictures, the child makes a connection between what they can see and the word for it. When there is no text, the child has more time to notice and think about details that could otherwise go unobserved, and this in turn presents opportunities for new words to come up. The parent or teacher can choose to highlight words for the child, repeating them and building them into the lead-up to a dramatic turn of the page. The adult can also support the child's understanding by asking questions about what has happened, or about what might be about to happen.

Involving children in the telling of a story

In a Spanish study which examined teacher support in storytelling, Cabrera and Martinez (2001) found that 10-year-olds understood a story better when the teacher not only made adjustments to the language they used but also involved the children in the telling, by asking questions to check their understanding. This includes questions about both what has happened and what might be about to happen. For example, in *Rosie's Walk*, by Pat Hutchins (1968), the reader follows Rosie the hen on her walk around the farm. Rosie is unaware that a fox is following her. Every time the fox pounces, he has an accident and misses Rosie. When reading this story with children, a teacher or parent might ask: 'What do you think is going to happen?' before turning the page. After the fox has failed to catch Rosie once, the children are likely to predict that this will happen again.

Developing cognition and language

Another advantage of picturebooks is that processing text and images makes simultaneous demands on the child, and this promotes the development of cognitive abilities. Since the pictures support understanding, the child can be exposed to more complex language than would otherwise be the case. Furthermore, with visual support, the reader's interest has a better chance of being maintained, always assuming, of course, that the story interests them.

Picturebooks can also stimulate language use and development through their design and typography. For example, readers of books that contain text may encounter a variety of font types, print sizes, block capital letters and use of colours in the words themselves. Writers of picturebooks also make use of 'endpapers' to frame the story. These are the pages which come immediately before and after the story itself. An opening illustration can prepare the reader for the story and can be exploited by the teacher or parent asking the child what they think the story will be about. The final endpaper presents an opportunity to reflect on what its contents add to the story once the actual telling is finished. Take *Zoo*, by Anthony Browne (1992), for example. The reader follows a family as they visit the zoo, viewing a succession of miserable animals in bare enclosures. On opening the book, the reader encounters a double-page spread that has a blank white page on the left-hand side (known as verso) and a blank black page on the right (known as recto). The same occurs at the end of the book. Questions to ask learners looking at the opening endpapers of *Zoo* might include:

- Why do you think these pages are empty?
- Why is one white and one black?
- Now look at the cover of the book. How do you think the endpapers are connected to the cover?

Having read the book with your class, you can ask them to think about the final endpapers and how these link to those at the beginning, to the cover, to the title and to the story.

Mourao (2016) notes that endpapers can be used to create a mood and argues that 'the very act of interpreting with others creates a real reason for the learners to use English' (2016:31). Even if the learners use their first language, they are exploring the world of the book, and learning new words in context as they draw on 'their previous knowledge of the world' (Mourao, 2014:78). Further, they are doing it together, which can promote a positive socio-affective environment in the classroom, which in turn has implications for learning.

The suitability of picturebooks for different age groups

Young primary-age children

For learners in the youngest age group, a wealth of books deals with such topics as health, education, energy, climate, and gender equality – many of which correspond to the United Nation's Sustainability Goals. These topics take the learners beyond second language learning and into the broader curriculum, presenting opportunities for cross-curricular project work. One example is *Welcome* (Barroux, 2016), where a group of polar bears sets out to find a new home. They are met with rejection on the grounds that they are too big. In the end, they find a place which is uninhabited and settle there. The book's title refers to the way in which the polar bears welcome new arrivals to their new home.

Common themes in books for younger learners include sharing, being a good friend, inclusion and celebrating differences. An example of a book which celebrates difference is *Giraffes Can't Dance* by Giles Andrae (1999). Gerald the giraffe is mocked by the other animals because he cannot dance as well as they can. But then a wise cricket tells him, 'But sometimes when you're different you just need a different song'. Encouraged, Gerald discovers his very own way of dancing. This amazes the other animals and leads Gerald to conclude that everyone can dance when they find music that they love.

There is much for children, teachers and parents to talk about in this book, but the main message is that, as human beings, we are all different and given the right conditions, we can discover our abilities. It is a book about accepting people for who they are.

Young children benefit from vibrancy and humour in books. The pictures in *Giraffes Can't Dance*, drawn by Guy Parker-Rees, are in vibrant colour, which highlights the heat of the jungle, the lush nature of the terrain and the visual differences between the animals who live there. The humorous drawings of the animals as they waltz, tango and cha cha illustrate for the child how these dances work. While the animals are shown dancing in couples, the final image is of Gerald, striking a solo disco pose, which both emphasises the humour and also underlines the self-confidence that he has now developed.

In younger learners, rhythmic, rhyming text presented in short phrases and sentences alongside images helps to support the acquisition of similar-sounding words; it also facilitates understanding of more complex language. In *Giraffes Can't Dance*, the text 'He was very good at standing still/And munching shoots off trees' appears alongside a picture of Gerald eating shoots and leaves from a tree. This is followed by 'But when he tried to run around/He buckled at the knees', with a picture of Gerald's legs giving way under his weight. *Munching*, *shoots* and *buckled* are not common words; the teacher might not want their learners to be able to use the words productively, but to understand them in context. The images make the meaning clear, and they might just lead the child to learn the word anyway.

Older primary-age children

At the next level, more challenging topics can be presented through the juxtaposition of text and pictures. The subject matter of some books for young L1 readers is still relevant to these older learners, and the text is not beyond their linguistic level. These books have a valuable role to play here. Browne's *Zoo* is an example of a book written for younger L1 readers that deals with a topic that is also suitable for older readers but at a simple linguistic level.

Another topic suitable for older primary learners is the refugee experience. For example, Sarah Garland's (2012) *Azzi in Between*, deals with the arrival's attempts to settle into a new life; Liz Lofthouse's (2007) *Ziba Came on a Boat*, focuses on the journey itself, describing how Ziba looks back to her old life, not knowing when or how her journey might end. Related to the refugee experience is that of cultural identity, relevant to the lives of children in multicultural societies. Ibrahim (2020) makes the point that 'the plurilingual children in our classrooms bring invaluable resources and knowledge of a linguistic and intercultural nature to their English language learning' (Ibrahim, 2020:14). Through exploring topics such as shared experiences, stereotypes and injustice or inequality, teachers can help learners of all ages to develop knowledge about and understanding of other cultures. Picturebooks have an important role to play here as the use of images can make clear for primary-age learners what words alone may not be able to do, especially taking into consideration their limited experience of the world.

Older learners and adults

Considering all the benefits of picturebooks in second language education, it is worth thinking about how they might also help older learners and adults. Exploring the world of a picturebook can afford opportunities for developing cognition, visual literacy (the ability to interpret images) and emotional literacy (understanding the significance of facial expression, posture and gesture) in all age groups. An example of a book suitable for older learners and adults is Shaun Tan's (2007) *The Arrival*, the story of a young man leaving poverty in his homeland in order to make a better life in another country. Without a word of text, but through sepia-coloured images, many of which represent fantastical beings, Tan depicts the daily struggle to establish oneself in a new land, the strangeness of the place and its impact on the new arrival.

Research support for picturebooks and illustrated books

A useful source of current research on children's literature in the second language classroom is the CLELE (Children's Literature in English Language Education) journal website. This section draws on some of the studies reported there and elsewhere.

Research conducted in classrooms with second language learners of various ages has found many benefits of working with picturebooks and books with pictures. For example, in a study with German 8- to 9-year-olds, Kaminski (2013) found that the young readers used the book's pictures to support their understanding and make plausible predictions about subsequent developments in the story. Despite having met the book only once, 12 months later they were still able to construct a timeline of events and remembered some of the words. Similar results were found with Swedish 11 to 12-year-olds in Ahlquist (2021), based on Dahl's *Fantastic Mr Fox*, which tells the story of three farmers who try in vain to kill the fox who is stealing food from them. One aim of this study was to investigate the extent to which the learners drew on the book's pictures as they read. While many were conscious of using the pictures to help them understand, some were unsure of whether they had used them. If the reader understands the text, there may be little reason to do more than glance at the pictures. On the other hand, a reader who does not understand the text may not necessarily think to examine the pictures for clues. This suggests that classroom work could usefully focus on actively drawing learners' attention to pictures in order both to support understanding and to develop lexical knowledge.

One way for teachers to do this is to embed tasks in the listening to, or reading of, a book (Ahlquist, 2020). This study was carried out with learners aged 10 to 11, and based on Dahl's *The Magic Finger*. Tasks that were embedded included jigsaw – arranging pieces of text in the correct order – as shown below (Figure 1.1). To do this, the reader has to make sure that the pieces of the narrative make sense together, drawing on linguistic clues at the end of one piece and those at the start of another – linking words such as *then*, *after that* or pronouns such as *he* or *she*.

Figure 1.1: Ordering sentences from the text

Figure 1.2: Predicting what might happen next

Predicting what might happen next in words and drawing was another task, as shown in Figure 1.2 above, where the word *duck* was unknown to many children at the start of the study.

Games such as bingo and crosswords were created based on the vocabulary of the book. The focus of this study was a core vocabulary of twenty words considered central to the book. I will return to this study in more detail in Chapter 5.

A year later, the same children worked with Roald Dahl again – *Fantastic Mr Fox* – with tasks that once more focused on the book's vocabulary but were also linguistically and cognitively more challenging than in the previous study. For example, the learners read a description either of one of the farmers' storehouses or cellar, and they drew their own picture based on their understanding. They then worked with a partner who had drawn from another description and took turns describing their version of the storehouse or cellar to their partner, who drew according to the instruction (Figure 1.3). The class teacher commented that, when they did this, the children realised how much they knew. Putting learners in situations where they can realise how much they know is potentially very motivating for them.

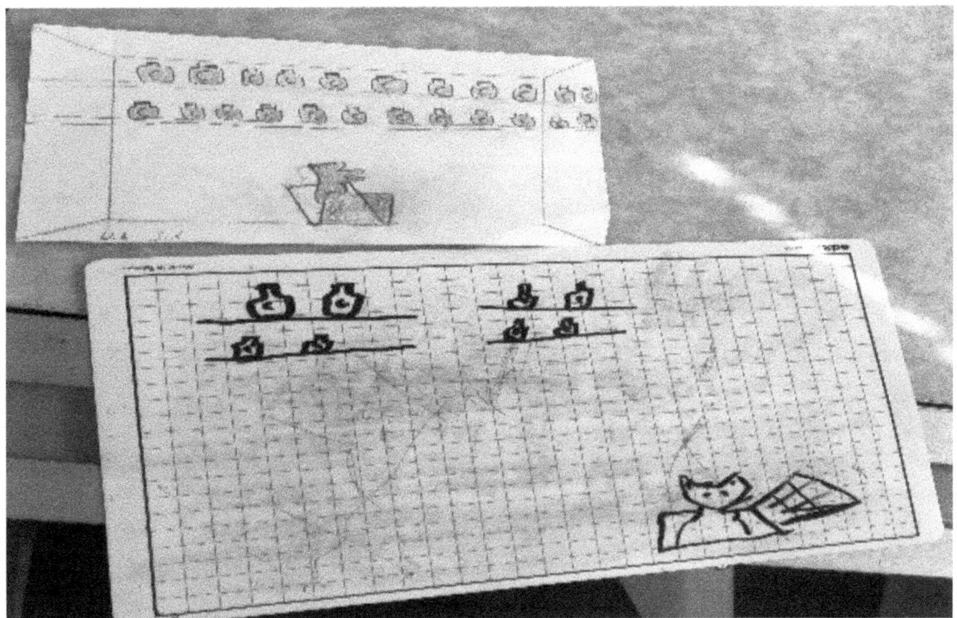

Figure 1.3: Comparing drawings with a partner

Practical applications

Blind Hand Description

This is best carried out when your learners do not know anything about the book they are going to work with. The aim is to create interest in the story and to encourage learners to start thinking about words which may appear in the book.

Time:	30–40 minutes
Age:	10–13
	10–11: children may need more preparation time
	12–13: some children may need more preparation time
Level:	Pre-intermediate
Key language:	Present tense (simple and continuous), articles, nouns, adjectives of description, prepositions
Preparation:	Decide which learners will work together in groups of four. Prepare four pictures from the book for each group. If you are working with a longer book, prepare four pictures from the beginning of the story; if you are working with a shorter book, prepare four pictures from the whole story.

Procedure:

1. Seat the learners in their groups so that they can see and talk to each other.
2. Place one picture face down on the desk in front of each person in the group. You can choose to give pictures with more detail to the more proficient learners. Say:

   These pictures are from the beginning of our new story. You are going to describe your picture to your group. Don't look at each other's pictures. Listen to each other and think about the order of the pictures. You can ask each other questions about the pictures. If you don't know a word, try to say it in another way.

3. Tell the learners they have five minutes to think about the words they need to describe their picture and write these down. Less proficient learners may want to write out whole sentences as preparation for describing their picture.

4. Learners take turns to describe their picture to the other learners in their group. Group members can ask for repetition and ask and answer questions.
5. When the group has decided on a possible correct order, they place the pictures face down on the desk in that order. The reason for placing them face down is that the learners have to try to reach a consensus before they go on to the next step. It is an opportunity for further discussion as they go over what they have said about each one to be sure of the sequence.
6. They turn the pictures over and make changes to the order if they wish.
7. Each child writes two or three of their chosen words on a sticky note and places this by the picture they described (still face up).
8. Each group tells the class about the story they have made from their pictures, using the sticky note words as prompts. They can do this either by coming to the front of the classroom and displaying their pictures on the whiteboard, or by sitting at their desks and telling their classmates the story they came up with. In this case, they might just hold up each picture as they talk about it. The children can talk about their own picture or you can ask them to choose a picture they did not describe. This depends on the proficiency of the learner and how much challenge you want for them or they want for themselves.

   If the lesson ends with the children sharing their own versions of the story, they will (hopefully) be curious now to find out about how the actual story plays out. In the next lesson, the learners place the pictures face up on the desk in the order that they decided on last time. You then read, or tell, the whole story or relevant part of the beginning of the book. If possible, use a projector to show the book's pictures as you read. The children rearrange their pictures, if necessary, as they listen.
9. For homework or in the next lesson, the children choose a number of words from those their group has collected and write them in their vocabulary notebook, each in a sentence, taking care to relate the sentence to the story. You might want to include words you think would be useful for everyone. If so, write them on the whiteboard. The notebook could look like this:

[L2 word] [sentence] **[L1 word]**

If the learner's first language is Swedish, it might look like this:

angry The girl is very angry and points her finger. **arg**

In this way, the learner not only has a story context to help them remember the word but also uses the word together with other words.

With a shorter book, this might be all you want to do, but with a longer text, or if you just want to work some more with a shorter one, then here are some suggestions for what you can do.

Extension:

If you are working with a longer book, give each group a large version of one of the coming pictures. Each group gets a different picture. Again, they start by thinking about the English words for things they see in the picture. Then you read or tell the story, pausing when it relates to one of the pictures. When a group thinks their picture matches this part of the story, one of them comes to the front and places the picture with a board magnet on the whiteboard. Once all the pictures are in place, ask each group to come to the front of the class and say something about their picture. Each member of the group should say something. This can vary from a sentence to just a word, depending on the proficiency level of the learner.

Variation:

If you have a lower-level class, instead of moving on just yet, you might want to do the extension task above by using larger versions of the pictures you used in the first lesson, rather than introducing new ones. This gives the children a chance to become more familiar with the words they used in the original task, where they placed the pictures in order in their groups.

Note: I learnt the activity Blind Hand Description several years ago from Lynda Baloche at a conference on cooperative learning. It is one of the most popular activities among my student teachers when we work with children's literature.

Professional development

Questions for reflection

- Think about the different stages of Blind Hand Description. How do you think they help the learners prepare for the story?
- Could you combine story work with another area of the curriculum? What might the benefits and challenges be?
- How would you feel about using picturebooks with teens and adults, and how might you do this?

Things to try

- Before they work with Blind Hand Description in English, get your learners to try it out in their first language so they can focus on the procedure. When the class have done it in their first language, ask them if they would do it any differently next time. When they come to work with it in English, remind them of what they said last time, and after they have done the series of tasks, ask them to evaluate whether it helped to have worked with them already in their first language.
- Organise a game of bingo or get learners to do a crossword based on some of the words that have come up in the story work.

Further reading

Birketeveit, A. & Rimmerheide, H.E. (2012). Does reading stories enhance language learning? In A. Hasselgreen, I. Drew, & B. Sørheim (Eds). *The Young Language Learner: Research-based insights into teaching and learning*, pp. 37–50. Bergen: Fagbokforlaget.

Ellis, G. & Brewster, J. (2014). *Tell it again! The storytelling handbook for primary English language teachers*. London: British Council, www.teachingenglish.org.uk

PEPELT website https://pepelt21.com/ for book suggestions and mini lesson plans.

2. Graphic novels

The terms *graphic novel* and *comic book* are sometimes used interchangeably, but there is a difference between them. While both use pictures and text to tell a story, graphic novels tend to be longer, with more complex characterisation and plot; the story is self-contained, with a clear beginning, middle and end. A comic book story might be part of a serial, to be continued in the next edition. Popular examples of comic book stories are Japanese manga and Korean manhwa, often published weekly and sometimes collated into books.

How a graphic novel works

In a graphic novel, a story is told using images, dialogue and narration in a series of *panels* – individual drawings with text – which follow sequentially one after the other, starting in Western literature from the top left-hand side of the page. Information is conveyed through the images and text, which usually complement each other. As the reader decodes the text and views the images, they construct meaning. Since not every detail or every event can be shown, the reader may need to fill in the gaps when moving from one panel to the next, as when watching a film. McCloud (1993) makes the point that graphic novels may also be intended to 'produce an aesthetic response in the viewer' (p. 9). This suggests an interactive experience which goes beyond reading, and which engages the senses in a way that is similar to viewing a piece of art.

The space between panels is known as a *gutter*. The writer uses the physical distance between panels to convey the extent of a time lapse: a greater or lesser amount of space can be left between panels to slow down or speed up the action. Wallner (2019) refers to the gutter as 'a space for reader sense-making' (p. 821), providing 'opportunities for readers to add their own narrative details, creating a story that transcends the panels and text' (p. 820). In other words, the reader of a graphic novel constructs meaning using the detail of the text, the images, the amount of space between the panels and, not least, their own imagination.

To add to the complexity of the experience, varying amounts of information may be shown in individual panels through sub-division into smaller sections. Further, as well as narration, dialogue and thoughts, there are often sound effects, conveyed using onomatopoeia – words which are associated with the specific sounds they represent: *boom*, *crash*, *screech*, for example. In addition, colour, the use of upper or lower case in narration and speech, and the type and size of font are some of the choices made by the writer and illustrator to convey meaning. Far from being an easy read, a well-written graphic novel can challenge a reader's understanding in many ways. Since there are as many genres of graphic novels as there are of novels in general, the graphic format can cater for a wide variety of audiences.

Graphic novels as a source of language

Some teachers are sceptical about using graphic novels in their teaching because there is limited text in comparison with chapter books, and they see them as presenting little linguistic challenge for stronger readers. However, the limited space available in each frame calls for precision in word choice and syntax. Although the reader may be faced with a small amount of text in each frame, it does not follow that this is automatically easy to understand. From one frame to another, the reader must decode the words and the images, and fill in the gaps between what is presented in one frame and what appears in the next. Doing this makes both linguistic and cognitive demands on them. If the learners then turn their attention to creating their own graphic texts, demands are made on their ability to express themselves succinctly in the L2. For older learners, discussion in L2 of how authors convey narrative and characterisation within the constraints of the graphic format promotes understanding of the genre and use of the technical terms mentioned above.

One way to gradually introduce the graphic form to your class is to work with hybrid graphic novels – books which provide running text in the way that traditional novels do, but with comic-strip-style illustrations. An example of a hybrid graphic novel is Jeff Kinney's popular *Diary of a Wimpy Kid* series, the first of which was published in 2007. The books tell the story of Greg, who, at the start of the series, is about 12. The intended readership age range is 8–12, with familiar, relatable themes, such as home life, sibling rivalry, school friendships and bullying. Part of the appeal for young readers is the fact that Greg himself is far from innocent in the situations in which he finds himself. His dilemmas offer opportunities for critical thinking and group discussion, with teachers asking questions such as: *What is Greg's dilemma? Would you do the same as Greg? Why / why not?*

Here are some more tasks, suitable for all levels of proficiency:

- Name five items Greg might have in his pocket.
- Work with a partner. Look at your partner's chosen items and say why you think your partner chose them. Were you right?
- Work with a partner. Write two lists of between five to ten words (adjectives and nouns):
  - How would Greg describe himself?
  - How would his classmates describe him?

The language produced in the above tasks is limited to words, specifically noun phrases and adjectives. However, in order to produce a response to the task, learners need an understanding of the character and the context. To do the tasks with a partner involves discussion, resulting perhaps in other insights. While the less proficient may not be able to have their discussion in L2, the focus nevertheless is L2 vocabulary, with implications for a deeper understanding of the text.

As you can see from the suggestions above, even where there is little text to read, a learner's lexical knowledge can benefit through the tasks that the teacher creates. In their book on how vocabulary is learnt, Webb and Nation (2015) discuss the various aspects of word knowledge, that is, what it means to 'know' a word. The first thing most people think of is meaning, but there is also spelling, pronunciation, how a word collocates with others (for example, *do your homework*, but *make a cake*), its level of formality and how to use it in a sentence. Webb and Nation also distinguish between *receptive* knowledge, when the reader understands a word, perhaps with the aid of context, and *productive* knowledge, where the reader both understands and can use the word themselves. In the task suggestions above, the starting point is a receptive understanding of the text's words in interplay with the images, but they lead the learner into encounters with other words. These may include words they already know receptively and are now going to use in their own production. These may be words they know in their L1 only, but now want to say in the L2. When they justify their choice of items that might be in someone's pocket, or list personal characteristics, the learner has to refer to the text, which requires close reading and attention to the words. The fewer words there are, the more attention the reader must pay to the story, and the more they need to read between the lines.

Graphic novels for all ages

Young primary-age children

For this age group, typical genres that are written at an appropriate linguistic level are graphic versions of fairy tales and medieval adventures, as well as stories of superheroes such as Batman, Wonder Woman or Superman. The benefits of graphic novels for beginner readers are likely to be found in the way the image supports understanding by showing the action, in much the same way as happens in a picturebook. The blurb on the back of the books in the Oxford Bookworms Starters series, for instance, states the publisher's intention: the graded stories are *supported by* the illustrations. Where learners meet unfamiliar words, they will look for clues in the images, aided by their imagination and that can be enough for the reading to proceed. But if not knowing a word prevents them from understanding the narrative, they can be encouraged to look it up in a print or digital dictionary, if these are used. Of course, the teacher can simply tell them what the word means in their L1, and that solves the immediate problem. However, looking a word up not only encourages learner autonomy, it also means that the learner is more likely to remember it, especially if they also write it in a vocabulary notebook.

Older primary-age children

Once children are able to cope with more text, opportunities open up for working with two versions of the same book: two graphic versions of the same story, or a graphic and a non-graphic version. Williams and Normann (2021) point out that the graphic novel of Neil Gaiman's *Coraline* is very similar to the original. The dialogue and narrative are largely unchanged, but the two books present a very different reading experience because of the choices that the illustrator has made.

Where there are two versions of a story available, the teacher can create comparison tasks which draw the learners' attention to differences and similarities in the text and images. One such task involves dividing the class in two, with one half reading the opening of the graphic novel, and the other half reading the opening of the chapter book. The learners then share what they know about Coraline and the setting from their version of the story. The class can be divided in different ways: one way is to have the less proficient pupils work with the graphic novel, where they will have the support of the images; alternatively, learners could be allowed to choose. Asking learners to select the version of the book they want to read on the basis of cover only is an interesting task in itself because you can ask them to explain why they chose the particular book. This task also makes for a good introduction to the story since it helps to arouse interest and expectations.

The risk here is that they all choose the graphic version, not just because they think it is easier to read, but because it is colourful and appealing (although not all graphic novels are in colour; some use only black and white images). Nevertheless, books which are aesthetically striking, attractive or intriguing are likely to appeal to young readers. I will return to *Coraline* when giving an example of practical classroom work.

In contrast to the vibrant colours of graphic *Coraline* are the stark black and white images of Marjane Satrapi's (2003) graphic memoir *Persepolis*. The main character is around the age of an older primary child (aged 10) at the start of the story, but the text is fairly challenging, linguistically, for most children of this age. The book recounts life during the Iranian revolution of 1979 as seen through a child's eyes. Its themes still resonate today: a society fractured by internal conflict, subsequent disruptions to everyday life, and the wrench of fleeing one's homeland in search of refuge elsewhere.

Both *Coraline* and *Persepolis* deal with issues to which older primary-age children can relate: family conflicts (both books); societal expectations and laws (*Persepolis*). You do not have to use the whole book; instead, you can select extracts to tie in with work in other subjects, such as civics or wider curriculum areas concerning themes of democracy, equality and personal freedom.

The two books mentioned in this section have been made into films and, as such, provide another medium as the basis for classroom work. Some of this could be done after the class has read the book, or while reading it, to bring focus to a particular scene. Some questions that can be used to frame the tasks are:

- What did you like most/least about the film?
- Which part of the book and the film respectively do you remember most clearly? Why do you remember that part so clearly?
- Does the film represent the characters and story in the same way as in the book? Write down three to five things you think are the same, and three to five things you think are different.

These reflective tasks can be done individually or in pairs or small groups, culminating in a whole-class discussion. Pairs and groups give everyone a greater chance of being involved and getting an opportunity to use the L2.

Even if the learners lapse into L1 in the heat of discussion, they will present their ideas to the rest of the class in the L2.

Older learners and adults

The graphic novel format is often associated with younger readers, but this is actually a Western perception. Manga – Japanese comic book stories or series – are aimed at both an adult and younger readership. For adults, there are also non-fiction titles, such as those that deal with topics such as business or biographies of historical figures. While some English translations are transposed to read left to right, other publishers retain the Japanese right-to-left format. This in itself creates a challenge which involves some adaptation on the part of the reader.

Raymond Briggs, best known for his children's books such as *The Snowman*, has also created stories with themes intended to appeal to an older readership. Examples are *Gentleman Jim* (1980), the story of a lavatory attendant who dreams of a better life; *When the Wind Blows* (1982), about the lives of a retired couple in a society facing a nuclear threat; and *Ethel and Ernest* (1998), the story of the married life, and deaths, of Briggs' own parents. Briggs' parents lived during the war and post-war years of the 20th century; this book provides a personal account of a period of history that learners may be studying.

Briggs' illustrations sometimes suggest an intended younger readership. If your older learners are put off by these, there are titles that might be more immediately appealing to them. For example, Guy Delisle's (2006) *Pyongyang*, originally written in French, depicts in black and white graphic form the way of life in North Korea as experienced by the author during a two-month stay, working as an animator. His books *Shenzhen* and *Jerusalem* chronicle in a similar way his time working in these places.

In fiction, there are graphic versions of classics such as Aldous Huxley's *Brave New World* (Fordham, 2022) and Harper Lee's *To Kill a Mockingbird* (Fordham, 2018), as well as original fiction such as *Banksy* (Matteuzzi & Maraggi, 2022), which is an imagined biography of the anonymous British street artist.

Research support for graphic novels

Krashen (2004) claims that graphic novels have the potential to develop literacy because they are fun, and this in turn motivates the reader to read other books. This seems logical, but it can be seen as diminishing the importance for language development of the graphic novel itself, in the kinds of ways I have suggested above. It also underestimates the work a reader has to do to make sense of a graphic novel. With space at a premium, texts are concise and words are chosen for their precision. With limited help from the text, the reader draws on the pictorial clues in the panels. Put simply, in order to construct meaning, the reader has to think.

Developing cognition

The role of thinking in the learning process is highlighted in the research on instruction through multimedia, which also involves both words and pictures. Mayer, who has written both on multimedia learning and the educational value of computer games (see, for example, Mayer, 2021), argues that for all meaningful learning to take place, three cognitive processes are required: selecting, organising and integrating. First, the learner selects the words which are relevant and processes them in working memory. A similar selection is applied to images. Secondly, verbal information (words) and non-verbal information (images) are organised (separately) in the learner's mind, and finally, the two are integrated, supported by the learner's background knowledge. Mayer refers to this process as 'sense-making' (Mayer, 2021:46).

While Mayer considers the cognitive processes to be separate but ultimately interconnected, Dutke and Rinck (2006) see them as occurring simultaneously; this, they argue, places demands on working memory. The significance of these differing views is that, regardless of whether image and text processing happen separately or simultaneously, graphic material presents cognitive challenges which should not be underestimated. As such, understanding (and learning) can be supported through using three types of classroom task: those which focus on text, those which draw the reader's attention to image, and those which bring the two together, resulting in deeper learning.

The role of the moving image in promoting learning should also be noted. Elsner and Viebrock (2013) compare the support readers gain from graphic material to that which they receive when watching television or playing computer games: in the latter, the visualising is done for them, freeing up capacity in the brain to concentrate on the text. There are readers who would prefer to do the visualising for themselves, but when the visualising is done for the learner, the teacher can build on what has been provided in the book and focus on developing language.

Promoting learner empowerment

In their book on using graphic novels in the classroom (see Further reading, p. 41), Jaffe and Hurwich (2019) note that the less proficient reader may be attracted to the graphic format because it is 'sufficiently different to empower them' (2019:61). By this they mean that the format makes the reader feel more confident and in greater control of their learning. Graphic novels enable the less proficient to read and understand a story through frames which display short texts of narrative, bubbles which show speech and thought, and clear illustrations of action and emotion. The reader does not have to hold a developing story in their mind as they read because it is there on the page, to be referred to if necessary. The positive experience of reading and understanding is likely to increase self-confidence and, in turn, the learner's willingness to graduate to chapter books.

The authors make it clear that graphic novels are not about 'dumbing down': in the graphic format, the need to be concise, together with the challenging word choices that come with this, can promote particularly close reading of the text. With fewer words to convey action or description, the reader has to predict, speculate, infer and deduce. While they are doing this, they are also required to interpret fonts, colour and layout. Finally, the aesthetic features provide scope for personal interpretation; this is engaging for the learner and helps to support them in processing the more challenging vocabulary.

Brinkman (2015) talks about empowerment in relation to her reading project with German 14 and 15-year-olds, using the graphic version of Anthony Horowitz's *Alex Rider – Stormbreaker*. The class had never worked with a novel in English at school. Language-based tasks in the project included drawing the pictures in blank panels where only the text was provided; filling in a form based on information given; reading a description, drawing a character based on it, and then comparing it with the one in the panel. Here, there is a combination of more traditional tasks, such as information transfer (filling in a form using the text information), and opportunities for creativity (drawing one's own impression of a character and then considering the similarities to, and differences from, the original). Before the project, the learners were instructed on the technical features of the graphic format – *panel*, *gutter*, *speech bubble*, etc. During the project, they discussed how the author and illustrator used these features in order to create a particular effect. They also had the opportunity to create panels themselves, applying their knowledge and discussing each other's work. Brinkman uses the word 'empowered' to describe how her learners felt confident to do these things, and the positive feelings which arose from the experience, leading many of them to want to read another book about Alex Rider.

One interesting point that Brinkmann makes is that some learners, when asked to reflect on the task they had just completed, were not sure they had learnt anything from it, even though they had enjoyed it. This highlights the need for teachers to know how to exploit the material in order to ensure that specific language learning goals are fulfilled – a point acknowledged by Jaffe and Hurwich: teachers may be reluctant to use graphic novels because they are not sure how to use them.

Working with the gap

Many of the tasks I have worked with in my career as a teacher have involved some kind of gap, providing a reason to talk, read or think, in order to solve some kind of puzzle. With graphic novels, the reader is continually filling a gap. McCloud (1993) expresses it as a 'dance' between what can and cannot be seen.

When learners read a graphic novel, they are presented with words and images telling a story, but not every part of that story is shown. This requires the reader to fill in the gaps themselves, and to do this, they have to understand what is provided in the text and images. In a study involving Grade 4 learners in an L1 context, Brenna (2013) considered how the reading of graphic novels could support the development of comprehension strategies. The study highlighted how teachers can exploit the filmic features of graphic novel images, such as the use of close-up, middle-view and distance shots to create a particular impression. Brenna attributes her students' interest in graphic novels to the richness of the materials, and writes that in their view, graphic novels make them 'think'. Examples of such thinking include how lettering styles and colour portray emotions, the reasons for using close-ups, and how the passage of time is conveyed. Close study of these features helped them to understand the book at a deeper level. Brenna notes that, because they were so engaged, the learners' discussions went beyond what might be expected for their age. This underlines the fact that graphic novels should not be dismissed as less serious, and again highlights how important it is for teachers to know how to exploit the materials to promote learning as well as enjoyment.

Working with the gutter, Brenna's students created drama sketches to depict the events that might have happened in between two panels. She points out that with the existing panels as a framework – the beginning and end of the action – the gap is filled, requiring 'careful thinking based on textual information' (2013:91). In a similar way, Jaffe and Hurwich (2019) suggest working with the gap by using the drama technique *tableau*. They claim that stronger students are challenged by working with techniques that are less familiar or unknown to them (such as *tableau*), and which require them to approach the material in a different way. *Tableau* demands close reading and interpretation of the text, resulting in a scene in which the learners use their bodies to form still images. Facial features, posture and different height levels are used to convey the panel's message. This can be presented to the rest of the class for discussion. It can also be extended to include the technique of *thought tracking*. Here, the teacher or a fellow student could touch the shoulder of a member of the tableau; this member then states the thoughts of the character they represent.

As learners progress through the school system, they move from learning about everyday life in the target culture to viewing it in relation to their own. Graphic novels may be able to convey this more powerfully than words alone. The notion of the unseen or unstated can prove especially useful where popular culture is concerned, providing an opportunity for developing critical literacy. Learners can reflect on what they understand of the foreign culture, in terms of how boys and girls act, or how different social groups behave (Huh & Suh, 2015). They can also consider how the culture depicted in the book seems different from, or similar to, their own.

Practical applications

Where and who?

This task is suitable for early readers and is based on the short novel *Escape* (Burrows & Foster, 2007, from the Oxford Bookworms Starters series). The opening scene shows a young man in a prison cell, frustrated because he is innocent. A prison guard arrives with his meal.

Age:	8–10
Time:	40 minutes
Level:	Elementary
Key language:	
Adjectives:	*sad, angry*
Nouns:	*man, prison, prisoner, cell, books, jug, window, door, bed, pillow, stool, sentence, guard.*
Verbs:	present simple: *is, opens, says;* present continuous: *is sitting, is reading.*
Preparation:	Check your school is licenced to copy, re-use and share content from a wide range of sources for non-commercial, educational purposes. Then photocopy and cut out the first seven panels; remove the thought bubbles, speech bubbles, and narration frames, either by cutting them out or by whiting them out with correction fluid. Put the learners in pairs.

Procedure:

1. As a warm-up, ask the children to look around the classroom and notice one thing in it. Go around the class inviting the learners to say their word. It doesn't matter if they say the same word as someone else. To increase the challenge, ask them to say whether any items were named more than once, and if so, which ones. More challenging still would be for them to accurately identify how many times the same thing was mentioned.
2. Give each pair the first seven panels and ask them to arrange these in the correct order. Next, ask them to decide where the story is set and who

the two characters are. They can discuss this in L1 but then prepare to say what they have decided on in L2.

3. Give the pairs the thought/speech bubbles and narration that you have removed and ask them to replace these. When they have done it, ask: *What do you know that you didn't know before?* (Answer: the reader has learnt the prisoner's name, the fact that he thinks he is innocent, and how long his prison sentence is.)
4. Give the pairs a copy of the book's short blurb in which the reader learns that the prisoner gets a very dangerous idea. Ask them what they think this could be. Create a mind map with the book's title *Escape* at its centre and the children's suggestions fanning outwards. Alternatively, write a list of the learners' ideas. Keep this until you have finished working with the book so that they can compare their pre-reading thoughts with what actually happens.
5. To round off, ask the pairs to turn the panels face down. Give them a minute to write down as many things as they can remember that are in Brown's cell. When the time is up, they turn the picture over and check to see if they have forgotten anything.

Extension:

Ask pairs to add up the number of things they remembered and to write the total at the bottom of the list. Then ask them to cover the list. Give them the same amount of time to write their list again, but this time, the aim is to add two more words. The important thing about this task is not which words they remember, but that they beat their previous total by two. If you think it would help them to look at the picture again before you start the second round, give them about 30 seconds to do so. When I work with the second round, I sometimes allow a little more time for the class to write their words (they don't know this) in order to give as many as possible a chance to beat their total. At the end, ask them if they managed to do this. Note that you shouldn't ask how many words each pair has remembered: the important thing here is that they beat the first total, whatever it was.

If they had previously remembered everything in the prison cell, they should aim to get the same items as before and to add two more things that they imagine might be found in a prison cell.

Comparing two versions

The following suggestion, suitable for an older age group, aims to capture the students' interest from the start of a book. It is based on the assumption that the class has already talked about the technical features of graphic novels: panels, gutter, speech/thought balloons, narration, sound effects, motion lines and background colours. The class should also have applied this technical knowledge in their reading of a graphic novel in their first language.

Time:	30–40 minutes
Age:	10–13
Level:	Pre-intermediate
Key language:	
Adjectives:	*dark, light, blue, yellow, green, brown, black, pink, long, scared, afraid, nervous, frightened*
Nouns:	*door, hallway, girl, hair, shorts, t-shirt, flip-flops, hand.*
Verbs:	present simple: *opens, looks, sees, stares, walks.*
Preparation:	Choose a panel from the graphic novel that you want to work with. This could be from somewhere in the middle. It should show enough detail to give learners something to talk about. For example, let's take *Coraline*. The book tells the story of a young girl, Coraline, who moves into an old house with her family. They live in just one part of it. One day, Coraline discovers a door and a hallway that leads to a house just like her own. The family that lives there is exactly the same as her own, but the new family allows her more freedom… until she tries to return to her real family. The book is considered appropriate for first-language speakers of English aged 8–12, but also to have appeal for older readers. Across one double-page spread, the graphic novel depicts the moment that Coraline opens a door onto a dark corridor which will lead her to the other family. This extract contains little text, but the wording is similar to the original version. In the original, Gaiman writes of a cold, musty smell coming through the doorway; it smells very old and very slow. In the graphic version, the reader

sees a half-page image of darkness with Coraline framed in a small doorway, illuminated by the light from her home. The same text is displayed in capital letters over four lines, like a poem. Below the large image, there are three small ones which show Coraline taking steps into the darkness.

Procedure:

1. As a warm-up, ask the learners to close their eyes and imagine they are opening a magic door. Tell them that you're going to ask them to name one thing that they see. They should keep their eyes closed. Ask everyone in the class. Learners listen out for whether anybody says the same thing, and if so, what it is.
2. Ask the learners to open their eyes and look at the panel. Ask: *What do you see? What do you learn from the text? What different colours do you see? Why do you think the author chose these colours? Why are the pictures of different sizes? What do you think this story could be about?* There is quite a lot to process here, so one way to approach this is to write the questions on the board and let them talk to a partner first.
3. Alternatively, if you have already set the scene and perhaps even read some of the book, the questions here could be: *What do you think is going to happen next? How might the book develop?*
4. Give them the short corresponding text from the chapter book, which describes how Coraline opens the door onto a dark, cold and smelly hallway and walks warily through the door; something about this place seems familiar to her.
5. Ask the learners about the similarities and the differences between the two extracts. For example, the images in the graphic novel tell us nothing about what is on the other side of the door – we learn from the text in the chapter book that it could be an empty flat. The graphic version does not state that Coraline was uneasy as she walked into the darkness, but perhaps the fact that there are three pictures devoted to her entering the hall is intended to convey the idea that she does this slowly and with some hesitation. In addition, the text in the chapter book tells us there is something familiar about the corridor, but this is not seen in the images in the graphic novel until we turn the page. Letting the learners talk in pairs here is a way to involve everyone, to allow them to notice details that individuals working alone might miss, and to prepare what they want to say. There is a limit to what learners in this age group are able to

express in the L2, but slowing the task down by allowing the children to talk in pairs supports their ability to do this.

6. To round off, ask: *What do you think Coraline is feeling and thinking as she walks into the hallway?* This could be expressed as a thought bubble:

I'm really cold.
It's very dark here.
I can't see anything.
I wonder where this
hall goes. I can't
hear anything.

What the learners might say:

Description: learners might say about Coraline: *She's frightened; She must be cold because she's only wearing shorts and a t-shirt; It's dark and she doesn't know what's there.*

Modal verbs: learners are quite likely to make use of modals here – *She could be scared; I would be scared; There could be a monster in the hall.*

Extension

1. Creating a prequel

   Learners work with events which precede the start of the novel and create a prequel. They imagine, for instance, what might have led up to Coraline and her family moving into the house. They create a storyboard (a sequence of drawings). Specify how many drawings and/ or how much time they will have for the task. They sketch out what they want each panel to contain in the form of text and images. This provides the framework and helps to structure the story.

2. Matching text with image

   1. Take the two pages which introduce the 'other' parents. Copy them and cut them up, removing the text so the learners see only the images. Ask what the reader learns about these people from the images.

2. Give the learners the text (the speech bubbles and narration frames). Ask them to arrange these in an order which makes sense to them. They do this without referring to the images.
3. Tell them that once they have an order that makes sense, they should match the text with the images.

This can be done in pairs or groups of three to ensure that all the learners are involved, and to give everyone a chance to use the language.

Extension

To set up a class discussion, copy larger versions of the images and place them on the board. Ask the pairs or groups to work together to make suggestions as to which piece of text should be placed against each image, and to justify their choice. In this way, attention is drawn first to the images, then to the message that is conveyed in the text, and finally to how the two work together. This is in line with Mayer's cognitive theory of multimedia learning, discussed earlier in this chapter. It promotes the relationship between words and the items they describe, thereby facilitating deeper learning.

If you have delved into the book as outlined here, rather than read from the beginning, you could at this point ask the learners how they think the book starts. They now know about this other family, which leads the reader to conclude that there must be an original family and that they live somewhere else in this house. This could form the basis for more work on the book: how did Coraline come to find this other part of the house, and what is it about her old life that at first contrasts rather unfavourably with the new one? As with all books, especially those for young learners, you may not want to work with the whole book. Instead, you could work only with the parts that develop character in some way or illustrate particularly dramatic developments, making use of some of the classroom activities mentioned in this chapter.

Professional development

Questions for reflection

- How did you feel about using graphic novels in your teaching before you read the chapter? To what extent have you changed your views?
- How would the age of your learners affect your choice of graphic novel and how you might work with it?
- Can you think of a cross-curricular topic you might work with that could include the use of a graphic novel?
- When you start to plan your work based on a graphic novel, what would be the most important things to think about?

Things to try

- Create a game to practise some of the words in the *Coraline* extract. Think about which aspects of word knowledge your game will focus on.
- Following on from the warm-up described in the 'Where and who?' task, ask the learners to draw a maximum of five things they would like to see when they open the magic door. They should include a thought bubble containing text that conveys what they are thinking when they see these things.

Further reading

Jaffe, M. & Hurwich, T. (2019). *Worth a Thousand Words: Using graphic novels to teach visual and verbal literacy*. San Francisco, CA: Jossey-Bass.

McCloud, S. (2001). *Understanding Comics*. New York City: William Morrow.

3. Graded readers

What is a graded reader?

A graded reader is a book that has been specially written to support second language learners. Although the focus here is English, there are graded readers for learners of many other languages. In English, there are genres ranging from novels (including graphic novels) to playscripts to non-fiction. As well as original titles, there are also adaptations of classics. What all these types of books have in common is that each title has been written for a particular level in terms of number of headwords (words which form entries in a dictionary), grammatical complexity and sentence structure.

One problem for teachers is that different publishers' grading systems vary: what might be deemed pre-intermediate for one series can be classed as intermediate for another. Some use the Common European Framework of Reference for Languages, or CEFR (2001, updated 2022). Others use this framework, but within it, they have their own subcategories. Ladybird, for instance, has no fewer than 14 levels for children aged three to 11. Eli-graded readers, on the other hand, have four stages up to A2 on the CEFR scale.

Teachers sometimes assume that graded readers written for struggling L1 learners are suitable for L2 learners. However, this is not necessarily the case. When an L1 learner starts to read in their own language, they have already acquired considerable lexical and grammatical knowledge, which they draw on as they read. They might try to sound out a word on the page and find they are able to match it to one they know in the spoken language, or they might use the immediate context to help them work out the meaning of a word they do not recognise. This is not the case for L2 learners, who have a much more limited bank of words to draw on in both the written and the spoken language.

Graded readers as a source of language

Graded readers for language learners gradually introduce the most important vocabulary – established by determining each word's frequency in the language. Readers' progress is affirmed as they move from one stage to another, coping with more words and more complex syntax. As well as providing material for reading at different levels, graded readers also offer opportunities for developing listening skills through e-book and audio versions of the text. Progression from one level to the next gives the learner an element of control over their learning and makes it visible both to themselves and their teacher. The sense of success experienced through completing a whole book is a source of motivation, which can encourage the young language learner to try books written for an L1 audience.

Let's take an example of a book written for L1 readers, *Prince Frog Face* (Umansky, 2015), which is intended for the 8 to 12 age group and is written for a reading age of 8. It contains idiomatic language likely to be familiar to L1 readers: *it all kicked off; clapped into a dungeon; staring daggers,* as well as the made-up word *blingtastic*, which readers might be able to decode through knowing the words *bling* and *fantastic*. Such expressions can present problems for L2 readers, although this depends on how much out-of-school exposure to English they have. Some of the young learners I have met in my research have a certain amount of familiarity with colloquial expressions (often acquired through gaming), but this is not the case for all. While idiomatic language is challenging for the young L2 reader, it might also be interesting for them to learn.

Let's now go on to look at what graded readers can offer second language learners of different age groups. As with any book, the graded reader needs to be able to offer an interesting story, with characters to whom the reader can relate and a plot that is not too complex, but not predictable either, and which perhaps includes moral dilemmas.

Graded readers for all ages

Young primary-age children

Engaging stories, offering readers the chance to use their imagination and form opinions, can be found at all grade levels. One example for younger children comes from the Penguin *Easystart* series, with 300 headwords. *Dino's Day in London* (Rabley, 2008) is a story of mistaken identity and impersonation. Dino, the son of a film star visiting London, is supposed to be taken on a taxi tour of the city while his mother is busy. When Billy, the same-age son of the taxi firm owner, finds out about this, he gets to the hotel early and goes off in the taxi with the pocket money intended for Dino. One task suitable for younger learners here involves them planning their own dream day out in London (or another city). To make this more challenging and realistic, there might be a budget, which would mean checking prices.

The learners could write a dialogue between Dino and the hotel receptionist, and, if they have worked with the past simple tense, go on to write Dino's diary for this day. The class might discuss whether Billy should have some sort of punishment, and what would be suitable. Billy could write a letter of apology to the film star.

Older primary-age children

Books written for levels up to and including A2 on the CEFR scale are likely to contain illustrations. Most primary-age children are around that level and are likely to find the illustrations entertaining and helpful in supporting their understanding.

Stories which include a crime or element of mystery often appeal to children of this age. Having both male and female lead characters can strengthen this appeal. One example from Oxford University Press is *Dead Man's Island* (Escott, 2000), in which a young girl and her mother go to work for a wealthy, mysterious man on his private island; this man has a secret, and the child decides to find out what it could be. Another book from the same publisher is *Death in the Freezer* (Vicary, 2007), in which sibling rivalry takes an unpleasant turn as one of the siblings becomes increasingly successful.

Teachers can access graded stories, as well as factual texts, for free on the British Council's website, https://learnenglishteens.britishcouncil.org/. The topics on offer on this website are likely to be of interest to older primary learners while still being within their linguistic range. (There is also LearnEnglishKids for younger learners – https://learnenglishkids.britishcouncil.org/.)

Older learners and adults

Older learners and adult L1 literacy learners can also benefit from graded readers. The Oxford Bookworms series, for example, includes age-appropriate books about famous people such as *Stephen Hawking* (Raynham, 2018), *Usain Bolt* (Raynham, 2019) and *Anne Frank* (Bladon, 2018). The series also contains fiction for the older reader in the form of adaptations of Sherlock Holmes short stories, Jane Austen's novels and the works of Shakespeare. Macmillan is another publisher which offers graded readers for the older learner, from CEFR level A1 up to B2 in a wide range of genres, most of which are also available in e-book and audio format.

Supplementary material

Graded readers also include exercises to check readers' understanding of the story's vocabulary, grammar and plot, which teachers might find useful to work with. In the Ladybird series, grammar workbooks provide practice to accompany their graded readers at different levels. For the older learners in this age group, activity books containing exercises that replicate the type of questions found in the Cambridge YLE exams (Roald Dahl's *The Magic Finger* is one example). The activities here encourage children to practise writing longer sentences with up to three clauses, more complex past and future tense structures, modal verbs and a wider variety of conjunctions.

If there is no separate activity book, publishers often include exercises in the books themselves for readers to work on before, while and after reading. These may be placed at the end of the book, or at various stages throughout it. The exercises are generally written in the same style as those in a coursebook and include questions about language issues and the story itself. Pre-reading tasks include predicting content based on the cover or blurb, matching words with pictures and listening to and matching descriptions with pictures. The exercises familiarise the learners with some of the book's vocabulary, but, just as importantly, they are intended to arouse interest and engage the reader by presenting situations that are relatable. At various stages, the reader will come across review questions, usually about characters or events. Typically, these take the form of multiple choice, true or false, or one-word/short-answer questions, requiring little writing. Answers to questions are not given in any of the books I have looked at, so it is always a good idea to go through the exercises carefully beforehand to be sure that you know what the correct answers are.

Tasks for older children might include considering what they would do in certain situations. One example is Helbling's *Mr Football* (Olearski, 2010), where the main character faces a dilemma. By way of introduction, readers are asked to use a scale to rate how likely they are to behave in a certain way, such as if something goes wrong, or if they have problems with someone at school.

Once they have read the book, to review their understanding of content and vocabulary, the learners might be asked to put sentences or events in order; they might match two parts of a sentence, or match a picture with a word, as in the pre-reading activity. They can be asked to fill a gap with a word or complete a sentence. There might be questions about the book's pictures, showing characters or events, or questions about how the reader thinks the main character has changed over the course of the book.

While-reading or end-of-book activities can also be used to practise and develop writing skills. For example, at the end of *Mr Football*, learners fill in a form using information provided in a short text about a footballer. This is an example of an 'information transfer' task that is sometimes included in coursebooks. Other tasks include writing a dialogue based on an event in the book and writing an email from the point of view of one of the speakers. As follow-up work, learners are encouraged to make a fact file about their favourite footballer (or another sports personality) modelled on the one they have read for the information transfer activity.

A useful supplementary feature offered by some publishers is an online diagnostic test, which enables the reader to find out the most suitable level for them regarding vocabulary and grammatical complexity. To support teachers, publishers' websites often provide extra resources, such as a guide to using the readers in the classroom, articles and interviews, creative writing resources, worksheets, tests and answer keys.

Developing learners' vocabulary

At the lower levels, authors provide vocabulary support for the reader as they read. Publishers handle this in different ways. Penguin prints new words in bold the first time they appear in the text, and includes a glossary at the end of the book. In *Mr Football*, glossed words are indicated as such in the text by a large blue dot, which some might find distracting, especially if they already understand the word. An alternative is to place new words and phrases, as in many coursebooks, at the bottom of the page on which they appear. One advantage is that this allows the learner to read a text at a slightly higher language level. They can quickly glance down, see what the unfamiliar word means, and move on. Putting new words at the foot of the page, however, is very much a short-term solution as these words are unlikely to be remembered if the learner only glances at them. Of course, receptive understanding in context might be sufficient, but if you want your learners to learn specific words so that they can eventually use them productively, try to create reasons for them to focus on the words and use them. This might involve making sure the words are included in the questions you ask and the answers you expect, or ensuring they come up in the course of a discussion that you initiate.

Research support for graded readers

Research into graded readers looks at three main areas: fluency versus language development, learning vocabulary and enjoyment as a motivator.

Fluency versus language development

If the purpose of a graded reader is to support reading and allow the reader the satisfaction of understanding and completing a whole book, then the advice to readers on the Oxford University Press website seems to make sense: choose a book just below your current level. In his guide to prospective writers of graded novels (see Further reading), Waring (2000) argues for the role of the graded reader in building fluency – the ability to read and digest the content of a text with minimal disruption caused by coming up against an unfamiliar word. Indeed, Waring places the graded reader within Paul Nation's (2007) model of the *four strands*. Over a series of lessons, Nation recommends an equal balance between four components: (1) input (reading and listening for meaning; (2) output (speaking and writing with meaning in mind); (3) accuracy or language focus (which might be related to lexis, grammar or pronunciation); and (4) fluency. Where the learner works systematically with graded readers, with the aim of improving speed and comprehension, this would include Nation's segments of both input and fluency.

However, Waring makes the point that, if the learner is going to learn new words or learn more about words they already know, then tasks should be just *above* their current level. Krashen (1982) uses the formula i + 1 to represent the relationship between reading material and the learner's proficiency level. The letter i represents the learner's current level and + 1 is one step up. However, if the reading material itself does not challenge the reader, then the teacher's tasks can provide the + 1 to which Krashen refers. From a teacher's perspective then, there are two issues here. One relates to graded readers as a way of developing fluency in reading, and the other as a way of developing language knowledge. My advice is to vary what you do: sometimes go for books which are slightly easier in order to boost reading fluency, and self-confidence, creating tasks to challenge your learners. At other times, choose books which, through the language used, will challenge them and facilitate learning of new language.

Learning vocabulary

When it comes to the learning of vocabulary through graded readers, an argument has long been made for the need for readers to meet the same words in different books written at a particular level (Wodinsky & Nation, 1988). This is based on the assumption that a reader needs to encounter a new word several times before they have a chance of remembering it. There is no agreed number of encounters in the research literature, but ten seems to be an average.

However, Waring and Takaki (2003) concluded that learners do not learn much new vocabulary from reading alone. As a learner of a second language myself (Swedish), I would agree. After many years in Sweden, I can read Swedish-language fiction and non-fiction with understanding, but my recollection of new words is poor, and perhaps not accurate, since I use the immediate context to help solve the problem. Of course, I promise myself to go back and look up the unknown words later, but I never do. The words I tend to learn are those where I really cannot work out meaning from context and have to ask about them or look them up. What I am talking about here is noticing words, or not. Schmidt's (2010) *noticing hypothesis* states that we have to consciously register a word in order to learn it – in other words, not just see (or hear) the word, but pay attention to it. When publishers highlight words in a text, they do so to attract the reader's attention so that they see and consciously register these words. You can also do this when you create tasks that draw your learners' attention to particular words.

In the UK, Macaro and Mutton (2009) conducted a study with young learners (aged 10–11) of French, in which the learners could not fail to notice words. The authors embedded L2 (French) vocabulary items (high-frequency function words) into a reader written in age-appropriate L1 (English). The point of doing this was to relieve the cognitive load so that the learners would understand most of the text and use this knowledge to work out the meanings of the embedded French words. They received instruction on how to do this. In the first chapter, 18% of words were French; once introduced, they were repeatedly used throughout the text. The percentage of French words increased with each chapter (for instance, 22% in Chapter 2). A second group worked with graded readers but received no training in how to infer the meaning of words from context. On subsequent vocabulary and comprehension tests, the authors found that the children who had received training on inferencing outperformed those who had not received strategy training. This led the authors to conclude that just 'exposing learners to text does not necessarily help them make informed guesses' (2009:175).

Enjoyment as a motivator

Macaro and Mutton report that the young learners involved in their study enjoyed working with the graded readers. This is important: as Krashen argues, when a learner experiences positive emotion, their affective filter is down and they learn. In the case of the learners in Macaro and Mutton, the novelty value added to the enjoyment. They had not worked in this way before. The same was true of the learners (aged 6–9) who took part in a two-year project in China. Accustomed as they were to working with coursebooks and practice drills (which offered little in the way of cognitive engagement or opportunity to practise higher-order thinking), the children found the reading 'purposeful and meaningful' (Qiang *et al*, 2020:278). The teachers facilitated learning through prediction of the story from the cover, jigsaw tasks and discussion about developments at certain points in the story. They found that their pupils improved in both speaking and writing, and they also noticed their enthusiasm about the books and motivation to work with them. This in turn had a positive effect on the teachers, which is a bonus.

Practical applications

In this chapter, we have looked at some of the ways that publishers of the graded readers provide practice in vocabulary and grammar. In this section, you will find ideas for adapting these tasks to the language level of your class.

Jumbled sentences

This is based on the jumbled sentence task included in some graded readers, in which the learners have to rearrange the words to make a grammatically correct sentence. In this task, the words are on separate pieces of paper. The advantage of this method over working with the jumbled words on a page is that the learners can manipulate the cards, moving them around as they change their minds. This is cognitively easier than trying to form, and hold onto, the sentence in their minds.

Preparation for a main task sequence to include in a 40 minute lesson (approximate timing 20 minutes):

- Choose three sentences from the book: one from the beginning, one from the middle and one from the end. Type them out in large letters, print them and cut them up so that each word appears on a separate slip of paper. To increase the challenge, use a longer sentence; for older children, include punctuation. For example, a sentence that might be suitable for a younger, or less proficient, group might be:

  Paul likes to meet his friends on Saturdays.

  A sentence that might be suitable for older children or more advanced learners might be:

  'Thank you, thank you', said Paul, as his mother gave him his favourite chocolate.

Procedure:

1. Put the learners in pairs and give each pair the three jumbled sentences.
2. The pairs work together to put the words of each sentence in the correct order. Now ask the pairs to write three sentences themselves – one each to follow on from those they have just worked with from the book.
3. If there is time, ask for volunteers to read out their sentences, including the original jumbled ones.

Variation:

Time: 10 minutes as a warm-up

Make a large card for each word in the sentence you have chosen and ask for volunteers to come to the front of the class. You need as many volunteers as there are word cards. For example, if the jumbled sentence contains six words, you will need six volunteers. The volunteers stand in a random order, facing their classmates and holding up their words. The classmates then have to rearrange their friends to form the sentence correctly. To structure the task and provide more time for processing, put the children in pairs and ask one pair at a time to suggest a move. Once the move has been made, everyone has a chance to review the new sentence before the next move is made. Seeing and naming classmates can have indirect benefits. For example, a classmate might say, 'I think Emma has to move next to David'. This can represent an important affirmation of a less visible child as a member of the class.

A task of this kind could take up a whole lesson, depending on the difficulty of the sentences in relation to the level of the class, but it is best to keep it short, using one or two sentences.

Kahoot

This is a popular digital quiz, which is free for teachers to use and quite easy to create. The website has guidance on how to do this. In Kahoot, a question is presented with four alternative answers. The learners click on their answers on their phones or tablets. After some time, the correct answer is automatically highlighted on the screen and the scores are displayed. The game can be made more exciting by reducing the time limit to answer questions, but it has to be reasonable in relation to the difficulty of the questions; otherwise, it loses its element of fun.

Time: 15 minutes (this could follow on from the jumbled sentence work described above)

Preparation: Create a Kahoot quiz based on the content of a book you have worked with or are still working with. Accounts can be created for free. An example of a question for the youngest learners might be to show a picture of a dog, with the text: 'This is a ____'. The answer boxes show the words *horse*, *dog*, *cat*, *bird*. For older learners, the same four words can be tested, but the pictures are replaced by a definition, such as: 'An animal that likes to eat hay' (answer: horse). Although the basic task is quite easy, you can increase the challenge by reducing the time limit, or by getting the learners to process a longer piece of text either in the question part or the answer.

As well as for reviewing vocabulary, Kahoot can work well for checking students' understanding of the narrative or descriptive content of the book, and the grammatical structures that have been used. Here you can use the sort of exercises which appear in the graded readers, for example, providing the first part of the sentence and giving learners four options to complete it. Alternatively, you could take a sentence from the book and offer four translation options in the L1. For older or more advanced learners, design the task so that there are only slight variations in the four L1 sentences.

Think about which learners you will pair or group together. In order to play, they need access to a digital device such as a smartphone or tablet – one per small group or pair.

Procedure:

Start by opening the Kahoot quiz you have prepared on the projector. The learners log in, using the game PIN that appears on the screen when you open your Kahoot. They create a group name, which appears on the screen. This helps you see that everyone is ready. They can choose to use one of their own names or make up a name for their group. If you decide to let them have a made-up name, they should choose this in advance. Not only does this save precious time on the day, but it also adds to the anticipation that the children are likely to feel.

At the end of the Kahoot quiz, there will be a winning group or pair. You might use a trophy, which is given to the winning group, and then passed on the next time you play Kahoot. Remember, though, that where there are winners, there are also losers, and the scores always appear on the screen. This might be a source of anxiety for some, and it is a good reason for using different pairs and groups whenever the class plays the game. Success is an important motivator, but so is learning. Ensure that you make time to go back over the questions and deal with any uncertainties; then recycle the questions in future Kahoot sessions. (Note that you cannot disable the timer function in a live game, but if you set the game as an assignment, you can. For some learners, the timer can lead to stress; for others, it adds to the excitement.)

Extension

Learners' own questions

Time: 10 minutes

This task might be used to start a lesson or round off the one in which you worked with Kahoot. Ask each pair or small group to go back to the graded reader and create a question in the same style that you used in the initial game, and four possible answers, including the one – and only one – which is correct. They write their question-and-answer options on a piece of paper and give it to you. Create another round of Kahoot using their questions.

Pack and dice

Preparation: For each pair or small group, create a pack of cards with keywords on them. The words do not have to be the same in each pack. Write on only one side of the card. The children can play the game in pairs or groups of three or four. Each gets a pack of cards and a dice. The pack of cards is placed face down on the desk. They take turns to throw the dice and pick up a card, which they hold closely to their chest so that the others don't see it. Depending on the number thrown, they do one of the following, and in doing so, practise different aspects of word knowledge, as indicated in brackets.

1. Say the word in L2 (pronunciation).
2. State the L1 translation for the word (meaning).
3. Draw the item on the card (meaning).
4. Say the word in a sentence (grammar).
5. State a word which is associated with the word on the card or which means something similar (meaning).
6. Describe what the word is without saying its name – in L2 if you can, otherwise in L1 (meaning).

If the player throws a 2, 3, 5 or 6, the other learner or learners must say what they think the word is. The player then shows the card.

If the player throws a 1 or a 4, the player shows the others the card and then speaks. The other team members say if they think what the player has said is correct or not. The teacher can be called if the learners disagree.

This is a fun way to review the words the class has been working with; it also allows you and your learners to build up a lexical resource over time, storing and adding to the cards as you work with different topics. The learners can help in the choosing and production of the cards. When there is a spare moment, they can collect a handful of the word cards and a dice, and play the game. Whenever you use it, take the opportunity to walk around the room and notice how well they know their words.

Professional development

Questions for reflection

- Plan a series of lessons on a graded reader. Create a number of tasks that will allow you to incorporate Nation's four strands.
- Choose a suitable graded reader for a class that you teach, thinking about the appropriate language level and topic for the class. Plan a series of lessons that help the learners to notice, and then use, any new vocabulary that comes up.
- What kinds of tasks or exercises that you already use could you adapt to working with a graded reader?

Things to try

- Next time your class is working on a project, choose a graded reader on the same topic, at a slightly higher level. Reflect on whether the project work provided support for the reading. Ask your learners what they think.
- All the tasks in the 'Practical applications' section focus on accuracy. To focus on fluency, choose a book that is slightly below the level of the learners. Once they have read it, task them with giving a presentation on it, acting out a scene or creating an interview with one of the characters.

Further reading

British Council on graded readers. Available at: https://www.teachingenglish.org.uk/professional-development/teachers/managing-resources/articles/using-graded-readers

British Council LearnEnglish Teens. Available at: https://learnenglishteens.britishcouncil.org/

Extensive Reading Central (2023). Writing a graded reader, by Rob Waring. Available at: https://www.er-central.com/authors/writing-a-graded-reader/writing-graded-readers-rob-waring/

Kahoot. kahoot.com

4. Fairy tales

A fairy tale is a traditional folktale that has been adapted and written down for children. It features fantastical happenings and characters. Common elements in fairy tales include a clear beginning and ending, a struggle between good and evil (represented in the nature and actions of the characters), and a conflict. There is an element of magic, often in the form of talking animals, a resolution to the conflict, which might come about through magic, and an ending in which good has triumphed over bad.

Fairy tales as a source of language

Within Europe, tales which are familiar to children in one country are often known to those in other countries, though sometimes under different names. When young learners are already familiar with a story in their own language, it is easier for them to understand as they read or listen in another language. They are familiar with the plot and characters, and therefore have greater cognitive capacity available to focus on the language. Even where tales do not have exact equivalents in other cultures, the stereotypes of the wicked stepmother, handsome prince and beautiful, down-trodden, heroine may well be familiar, as may the traditional opening and closing phrases of many stories: 'Once upon a time', and 'They lived happily ever after'. Nowadays, fairy tales are perhaps better known to children the world over through the many Disney versions, which fill our screens with images of beautiful maidens, handsome heroes and evil-doers of all kinds.

The main criticism levelled at traditional fairy tales is their tendency to stereotype, particularly where gender is concerned: females are depicted as weak and males as powerful and adventurous. We will look at ways in which some publishers deal with gender issues later in this chapter. Another criticism often made by language teachers is that many of the words do not fall within lists of the most common words in English, so the vocabulary learnt is often not much use 'in real life'. Examples of such words are: *wicked*, *stepmother*, *handsome*, *castle*, *witch*, *poison*, *cruel*, *dwarves* and houses built of *bricks*, *sticks and straw*. However, since stories like these play such an important role in many children's worlds, it could be argued that it is the corpora on which the frequency lists are based that are lacking.

In any case, fairy tales contain a wealth of everyday vocabulary and other language features that can be explored in class – topics such as animals or family, and grammatical areas such as prepositions and past forms.

Despite the criticisms, fairy tales remain central to children's imaginative worlds and continue to play an important part in the early days of listening to stories in their first language. The ongoing popularity of fairy tales is acknowledged in the fact that they feature significantly in graded readers for second language learners.

The suitability of fairy tales for all ages

Younger primary-age children

For the youngest learners, the familiarity of fairy tales provides a safe and fun way into English, with the many updated versions maintaining the fundamental values of the original tales. Written for 3 to 6-year-old first-language readers, Babette Cole's *Princess Smartypants* (1997) tells the story of a very modern young woman who really does not want to get married, and so sets her suitors impossible tasks in an effort to remain independent. The subversion of the traditional tale in which the handsome prince wins the hand of the beautiful princess and they live happily ever after is likely to appeal to L2 readers who are starting to read in English. The illustrations make the meaning of the (limited) text clear enough for younger L2 readers, and a more recent version of the story (*Princess Smartypants and the Fairy Geek Mothers*, 2017) brings it into the digital age: the princess helps to solve the problems caused when a website selling wishes online goes wrong. A useful resource for language work at this level is the British Council's LearnEnglishKids, which provides traditional fairy tales adapted for young L2 learners, with resources including worksheets, videos, and word games.

Older primary-age children

Older primary-age learners are beginning to be able to see things from other perspectives, developing their emotional intelligence (that is, an awareness of their own emotions and the ability to use this self-awareness to empathise with others). At this stage, older children can enjoy and benefit from fairy tales that are told from another angle, as in *The True Story of the Three Little Pigs* (Scieska, 1991). Here, the wolf is the narrator, telling his story from prison. He claims that he has been falsely convicted, following a series of accidents that led to the death of the pigs. A sense of the rather cocksure personality of the wolf comes through in both text and images. This also comes across well in the reading by the author himself, which you can find on YouTube. The scenario lends itself to a variety of language tasks, such as newspaper or television interviews with the wolf, a letter from the wolf to his mother, a diary extract, an account of his daily life in prison, or a list of requests to the prison governor to make his life inside more comfortable. Similarly, *The Other Side of the Story*, published by Picture Window Books for 4 to 8-year-old L1 readers, offers a whole series of well-known fairy tales from another character's perspective. Once your pupils have read some of these stories, they might like to try writing one of their own, such as *Snow White* from the perspective of the queen, or *Hansel and Gretel* from the point of view of the witch.

Aimed at the same age group, *Telling Stories Wrong* (Radari, 2022) provides an alternative way of telling a story. In this book, a grandfather tells the story of *Little Red Riding Hood* to his granddaughter but keeps getting the details wrong, and she has to correct him. This is a good way to review a story you have read to your class: change a few details, but not too many or too often so as to avoid detracting from the flow. Tell the story without interruption and get the children to note down, or try to remember, what was different. You might tell them that you are going to change three things, so they must listen carefully. To support them, you could create a worksheet with pictures from the story on which they have to put a tick or cross as they listen.

As well as stories told from other perspectives or containing incorrect details, there are stories that constitute different versions of traditional tales for children. One example is Eugene Trivizas' *The Three Little Wolves and the Big Bad Pig* (1997), a reading of which is also available on YouTube. The series *Seriously Silly*, aimed at first-language readers aged 6 to 9, offers humorous modern takes on familiar stories, which are likely to appeal to many older primary-age readers. The series includes *Cinderboy* (Anholt, 2002a), the tale of a young boy, bullied by his stepbrothers. Although he is as passionate about football as the rest of the family, Cinderboy always has to stay at home while the others go off to watch the matches. However, with the help of a fairy godmother, Cinderboy gets to play in a major football match, losing one of his boots in his hurry to get home before the magic fades. The story ends happily when the coach of the national team tracks Cinderboy down as the wearer of the boot. If your learners enjoy this book, they might like to read *Snow White and the Seven Aliens* (Anholt, 2002b), which is about a pop group.

Older learners and adults

Many fairy tales were not written with a child audience in mind: some of the Grimm brothers' tales, for instance, contain characters and events that are particularly dark. One example is *Hansel and Gretel*, in which a wicked witch attempts to fatten up the young boy, Hansel, in order to eat him. And this is after the father, in thrall to his new wife, has abandoned his children alone in the forest.

Though the stories were written for children, Roald Dahl's *Revolting Rhymes* can still be appreciated by an older audience. Six traditional tales are retold in rhyme, offering twists to the stories they are based on, with the kind of dark humour which characterises many of Dahl's novels. The endings are often changed in ways the reader least expects. At the end of *Little Red Riding Hood*, for instance, the girl comes face to face with the wolf and takes out her pistol.

Countering the issues of gender stereotyping and sexual orientation in fairy tales

Through fairy tales, teachers can explore ideas around gender stereotyping and sexual orientation with all age groups. In *Neither* (2018), Airlie Anderson presents a world which consists of blue bunnies and yellow birds. When a newly born creature tries and fails to fit in, it leaves and discovers a place where there are creatures of all kinds. This is a board book (mainly pictures, with few words), aimed at the youngest L1 readers. Slightly older, but still in the under-8 L1 reader age group is *Julian is a Mermaid* (Love, 2018). This tells the story of a boy who, inspired by the sight of three women decked out as mermaids, wants to create his own costume, but wonders if he will be allowed to do this.

Same-sex relationships are a theme in the work of Olly Pike. In *The Prince and the Frog* (2018), intended for 3 to 7-year-old L1 readers, the prince has been turned into a frog, and, as in the original fairy tale, is going to be returned to human form by a kiss. But in this tale, a brother and sister both want to help, and the question to be resolved is which of them will be the prince's true love? The world depicted in this book is one of acceptance, and the same is true for Pike's *Prince Henry* (2020), aimed at a slightly older L1 readership. When Henry reaches marrying age, his parents invite both princes and princesses as possible marriage matches to meet him.

For L1 readers aged 12 and over, *The Royal Heart* (McGoon, 2015) features a transgender protagonist. The King and Queen prepare their male child to take on the responsibilities of kingship. But as he grows up, the boy becomes less sure of his identity and leaves the kingdom. At the end of the book, he is magically transformed into a princess, and returns home, to be accepted by the King and Queen as their successor. For more LGBTQ fairy tales see Mombian (2023).

The website 'she reads' is a useful resource for reviews of young adult feminist novels. These include modern retellings of traditional fairy tales, such as *The Princess and the Fangirl: A Geekarella Fairy Tale* (Poston, 2020), based on Mark Twain's *The Prince and the Pauper*. The original is a tale of mistaken identity, in which a poor boy and a prince accidentally change places and have to face various challenges in their new lives. Poston's version tells the story of two feisty young women (an actress and a fan) who change places and team up in a race to find a leaked television script, dealing with a series of seemingly impossible challenges.

Another book that turns a fairy tale upside down is *All the Ever Afters: The Untold Story of Cinderella's Stepmother* (Teller, 2019). This is the story of Agnes, the woman who marries Cinderella's father. The author, who became a stepmother herself, explains that, through Agnes, she wanted to take the stereotype of the fairy-tale wicked stepmother and present a more nuanced view. In this story, Cinderella, though good-hearted, is rather a spoilt, precocious child who tests the patience of her stepmother. While Agnes generally acts with the child's best interests at heart, she struggles to love her. In later years, she questions whether there were times when she acted unfairly towards Cinderella. However, the story ends happily for all, with Agnes and her daughters, with whom Cinderella has a warm relationship, living at the palace.

Getting started on fairy tales with your class

While fairy tales have a lot to offer all age groups, the teacher's challenge is to get older learners interested in working with them, since they may consider them to be more suitable for younger children. Let's look at how you might do this.

Prepare by selecting one fairy tale per group of three or four. For example, if you have six groups in the class, you will need six fairy tales. Download summaries of the stories from a resource such as *The Summaries of 150 Classic Fairy Tales* (De Fabris, 2014). Write the name of a character from each fairy tale on a card.

1. Put the children into groups of three or four.
2. Give each group just the titles of the tale you have chosen for them. Tell the groups they have five minutes to tell each other what they know about the story.
3. Give out the summaries you have prepared, ensuring that they match the titles the groups already have. The groups check what they have said against the summary and tell the class if there was anything they remembered differently, or not at all.
4. Give the name of a character from one fairy tale to a group that worked with a different tale. For example, you might give the handsome prince from Snow White to the group that worked with *Goldilocks and the Three Bears*. The groups now have another five minutes to create a retelling of their story which includes the new character. They then tell this to their classmates.

This task introduces the idea of subversion, or 'trouble-making', whereby the new character comes in and disrupts the status quo by changing the traditionally accepted story.

Research support for fairy tales

In his article on the cultural and linguistic benefits of the fairy tale, Simon (2022) highlights the fact that because fairy tales are familiar to learners, they can be more easily understood: 'Once the student recognizes the evil queen, all words and actions she displays are set in a pattern students already expect' (2022:3). Because the traditional versions of fairy tales are familiar, the learner's attention can be directed to words and the way they are used. This is made clearer through the concreteness of the context in which the words appear. Simon further notes that fairy tales are 'for the most part, self-contained, without requiring an extensive amount of outside information' (2022:2). They are also often short, which he sees as a benefit in the digital age, when readers' attention spans may be limited.

Similar points are made by Koushki (2019): fairy tales are suitable for the language classroom due to (1) their brevity, (2) the fact that they are syntactically simple, making them more accessible, and (3) their ability to arouse learners' enthusiasm in a way that coursebook materials sometimes do not. Learners are exposed to grammatical patterns and vocabulary in context, with repetition of words and phrases. She argues that fairy tales present examples of emotions we can all identify with – love, happiness, jealousy, fear, uncertainty – and that they 'illustrate universal values for life' (2019:144). All of this offers opportunities to work with emotional intelligence through discussions, games and drama.

Many classic fairy tales have been adapted as apps. Someone who has written widely on the benefits of literature in the language classroom is Janice Bland. She has compiled an annotated bibliography of recommended reads for primary and secondary learners (2015) and has evaluated the benefits and drawbacks of story apps, many of which feature fairy tales. When the reader meets the story through an app, they encounter not only text but animation and different character voices, as well as that of the narrator. In addition to being multimodal, story apps are interactive, often giving the reader a chance to influence developments in the story. Bland (2018) gives an example of *Jack and the Beanstalk* (created by Nosy Crow and Ed Bryan, 2015). At the top of the beanstalk, Jack finds the giant's castle and a choice of doors. The reader has to choose the doors for Jack and carry out different tasks to help him. Bland makes the important point that 'through these challenges that relate to both linguistic and content-related aspects, the story app is still interesting for students who may have grown out of the typical fairy tale age' (2018:107).

Research shows that story apps offer benefits in terms of increasing motivation to read and engagement with the text. However, one downside is that interactive features can be distracting and disrupt the reading process. Bland's own work has reported similar findings. In a study with German 8 to 11-year-olds, she found that learners were helped by hearing the audio as they read, and seeing the words highlighted on the screen as they were read out loud by the narrator. Understanding was also supported through the use of distinct character voices, as well as clickable and moving images. The level of support provided meant that learners could read more advanced texts than they might otherwise have been able to do. Bland also found that the young readers developed their ability to predict, make inferences, and revise assumptions as the story progressed.

On the downside, the study also found that some animations occurred too quickly, giving the reader little time to digest the text. Animations proved most useful when the reader could activate them in their own time. Perhaps inevitably, some of the young learners were more interested in the animations than in reading the story. Bland's conclusion is that story apps are useful, but pupils need direction when they work with them. This can take the form of tasks to work on before-, while-, and post-reading; ideally, they should draw on the readers' own experiences and opinions.

Practical applications

In this section, we will work with the concept of 'noticing'. The task assumes that the class is already familiar with the past simple. It can be used to introduce the past continuous form.

Age: 11–12

Time: 40 minutes

Language focus: past continuous

Preparation: On the whiteboard, write the following, using two colours or styles:

was snowing

was reading

were sitting

was drinking

was thinking

ran

threw

heard

shouted

shook

At the top of another part of the whiteboard write: **This is a story about three little pigs**.

Procedure:

1. Tell the class they are going to listen to a short story that contains the verb forms that they can see on the whiteboard. Before they listen to the story, they should write these in their books or on a piece of paper. They do not need to use different colours.
2. Explain that you are going to read them a short fairy tale. They must number the verb forms in the order that they hear them.
3. Read the story below.

   This is a story about three little pigs. One night they were sitting by the fire. It was snowing heavily outside. One pig was drinking hot chocolate. Another was reading a newspaper. The third was thinking about dinner. Suddenly they heard a loud noise. The door shook in its frame. Someone shouted 'Help, it's cold out here!' The oldest pig ran to the window. He threw out an old wool blanket.
4. Learners check their answers with a partner.
5. Ask the learners which verb form they heard first, second and so on. Write these in the middle of the whiteboard under the sentence 'This is a story about three little pigs'. As you do this, the learners should also write the correct order down the middle of their page.
6. Tell the learners that you are going to read the story to them again. This time they should try to remember the words that go *around* the verb forms, and write them down after you have finished.
7. When you have finished reading the story out, the learners write down what they can remember, around the verb forms, as shown below. You could repeat this stage to give them a chance to listen for details they may have missed.
8. The learners compare their answers with a partner.
9. After a few minutes, ask the learners to help you complete the story by telling you what to write around the verb forms on the whiteboard. If they do not remember the details, or they remember other things, it does not matter, but you write up only the original story. It should look like this. (Note that I am not using punctuation in this task in order to keep the focus on the verb forms.)

This is a story about three little pigs
One night they ***were sitting*** by the fire
It ***was snowing*** heavily outside
One pig ***was drinking*** hot chocolate
Another **was reading** a newspaper
The third ***was thinking*** about dinner
Suddenly they **heard** a loud noise
The door **shook** in its frame
Someone **shouted** help it's cold out here
The oldest pig **ran** to the window
He **threw** out an old wool blanket

10. Now the class reads the story out loud together with you. Repeat this choral reading a couple of times, asking them to make it sound dramatic – they can stand up to do this. For the final telling, rub out everything except the verb forms and ask the class to help you tell the story one more time. Having repeated this a few times, the learners will be prompted by the verb forms to remember the rest of the sentence. The verb forms are now left in focus on the whiteboard.

Learning is supported in two ways here. Firstly, colour is used to highlight grammatical structures or words that you want to draw attention to. Start by asking them why you have used two different colours. Visually, this is fairly clear: there are two different verb forms. Secondly, ask learners to verbalise their understanding of *why* there are two different verb forms. If the children are able to express (in L1 most likely) that the first five verb forms set a scene, and the second five describe interrupted action, you will know that they have some understanding of when the past continuous form (not yet referred to by name) is used. How hard this is for them may depend on how this contrast is expressed in their first language.

In the next lesson, in pairs, give the learners a title and ask them to write a short story using the same five *was/were + ing* forms and the same five past simple forms (though not necessarily in the same order). Either write these on the whiteboard or, better still, ask the learners if they can remember which verbs and verb forms were used in the story about the little pigs. The title I use for this task is *The Silver Shadow*. The learners first have to decide who or what is being referred to in the title.

Though my example here is for older primary-age children, the same task can be used with younger children to contrast the present simple with the present continuous. After all, stories, including novels, often use the present tense for narration in order to give a sense of immediacy and drama. The words and phrases which surround the verb forms can be made easier or harder. The task involves listening, writing, focusing on language and reading aloud. To build in more reading aloud, invite pupils to tell their own stories to their classmates.

Extension:

So far, we have worked with a controlled text (*Little Pigs*) and a guided text (*Silver Shadow*). Now it is time for the children to apply their understanding in a story of their own, choosing their own verbs. The children's own story will be based on a picture that you provide, perhaps taken from a site with free-to-use images. They can write individually or in pairs, but the requirement is the same: they should use five verbs in the continuous form to set the scene, and five verbs in simple form to describe the actions.

For learners who need some help coming up with ideas for a story, provide more pictorial support. For example, let's imagine that the learners are going to write about the Smith family's day out at a local wildlife park. Here's what you do:

1. Find a picture of a family visiting a wildlife park, showing at least five animals, and display it to the class.
2. Ask the learners to tell you what the people and the animals are doing (this sets the scene).
3. Now tell them that suddenly there is a clap of thunder and it starts to rain heavily (if you can make use of sound effects here, even better).
4. Ask what they think the people and animals do next.
5. Note that so far, the present continuous and simple have been used. Examples: the giraffes are eating leaves; the giraffes stop eating.
6. Now say that the family are back home and talking to their neighbours. They tell them about their visit to the wildlife park, structured as shown below. Write these two sentences on the whiteboard and ask your learners to copy them into their notebooks:

   This afternoon we went to the wildlife park. There were lots of animals.

7. Write the instructions for the writing task on the whiteboard to remind them what they have to do:
    - Use five verbs to set the scene (past continuous)
    - Write: **Suddenly, there was a clap of thunder and it started to rain heavily**.
    - Use five verbs to describe what the animals did next (past simple)

A text might look something like the one below, but do encourage your learners to use their imagination - this could be easier for them if they work in pairs.

> *The giraffes were eating leaves. The lions were sleeping. The zebras were standing together. The monkeys were climbing the trees, and the hippo(potamus) was splashing in the lake. Suddenly, there was a big clap of thunder and it started to rain heavily. The giraffes stopped eating. The lions jumped up. The zebras started to run around the field. The monkeys screamed in fear, but the hippo(potamus) just splashed and looked happy.*

Variations:

1. The 'Three Little Pigs' text can also be used as a dictogloss. In dictogloss, the learners listen carefully as the teacher reads out a text. They do not write as they listen; instead, they try to remember words and phrases from the text. Once the teacher has finished reading, the learners write down as much as they can remember. Next, they work with a partner to reconstruct the text further. Calzada and Garcia Mayo (2020) have described the technique as a useful way to highlight a grammatical structure in a meaningful context, and also a way into L2 writing, which can be daunting for many learners. Working together with a partner can relieve some of the anxiety and boost chances of success, as can the fact that the writing itself is more limited and does not require free production.
2. An alternative variation is to use the continuation of the story (see below) as a dictogloss to review the two grammatical structures at a later date. In this version of dictogloss, the learners will eventually have an exact copy of the text you read out to them, not just the text they manage to construct with their partner, as in the previous example.

Story continuation:

The wolf looked in surprise at the blanket,
and called out again to the pigs.
He was shivering, his teeth were chattering,
he wanted to build a fire with twigs.
He banged again on the pigs' door,
and said in his loudest voice,
'Let me in or I'll blow your house down,
It's up to you – it's your choice!'

Preparation: For this, you need three versions of the gapped text in Appendix 1. Each version has gaps in different places.

Procedure:

1. Tell the learners that the story you are going to read to them follows on from the one they worked with before. Ask: *Do you remember how that ended?* Tell them that when you have finished, they will have written the same words that you have in front of you. Tell them there are several stages: the task starts individually and becomes a pair work task, and then a group task.
2. The learners listen as you read the story aloud. They listen and try to remember some of the words and phrases.
3. When you have finished reading, they write down what they can remember. The use of rhyme in the text helps them to do this.
4. Read the story aloud a second time. When they listen again, they note down any words they may have missed.
5. Next, the learners work with a partner to try to reconstruct the story further.
6. Give each pair one of the gapped versions of the text, which they complete using their notes. Each gap contains one word. (A contracted form counts as one word.)

Remind the learners what you said about having the same words as those you read out. Ask: *Do you have the exact words I read out?* The answer to this is usually some uncertainty.

The learners do not yet know that the gaps were in different places in the various texts they were given. Now bring together three pairs who have each had a different version. Between them, they will have the exact words that you have. Ask them to check their version by talking to each other.

There are two particularly positive aspects to this way of working with dictogloss. One is that there is no room for argument since every word of the story is in one or other of the versions. The second point concerns observing the strategies the learners use in this final stage. Watch what they do and note any strategies they use. Do they take turns to say the words? Do they have a final read-through so that everyone is satisfied? With your learners, review any strategies you have observed by asking them to think about how they worked with the final stage and if they were confident that they had the exact copy of your original story.

Professional development

Questions for reflection

- Do you think that fairy tales are a useful source of vocabulary? How might you work with the vocabulary of fairy tales in a non-fairy tale context?
- In what ways might your learners benefit from working with a fairy tale app?
- In the dictogloss task, the learners first attempt to reconstruct the text with their partner, and only after that are they given a gapped text to complete. What do you think is the benefit of letting them try to construct the story before they are given the gapped text?

Things to try

- Based on your classroom work with fairy tales, ask your learners to compile a database of fairy tale words. If they do this in groups, they can then compare the words they have chosen. Do the same yourself and compare your words with theirs.

Further reading

Bland, J. (Ed.) (2015). Annotated bibliography: Literary texts recommended for children and young adults in ELT. *In Using literature in English language education: Challenging reading for 8–18-year-olds*. London: Bloomsbury, pp. 277–299.

Mombian. (2023). *The Mombian database of LGBTQ family books and more.* https://mombian.com/database/

shereads (2023). Young adult (book list). https://shereads.com/category/book-lists/ya/

Wright, A. (1997). *Creating stories with children*. Oxford: Oxford University Press.

Wajnryb, R. (1990). *Grammar dictation*. Oxford: Oxford University Press.

5. Novels and short stories

A novel is a book that tells a story about imaginary people and events. There are many different genres of novel, for example, romance, comedy, thriller, horror, science fiction and historical fiction. Novels come in different lengths and complexity of plot; they employ the past or present tense for telling the story and include greater or lesser amounts of dialogue and description. The plot unfolds through the eyes of a first-person narrator or a third person who may or may not be involved in the story. Short stories are, by definition, shorter than novels and less complex, but have clearly established settings, characters and themes.

For a teacher wishing to work with a novel or short story, there is a huge amount of choice. This is a great thing, but where should you start? One possibility might be to start on a small scale, with a short story taken from an edited collection or from a collection of stories written by the same author. Let's consider the benefits for second language development of working with novels and short stories in the classroom.

Novels and short stories as a source of language

On the face of it, starting with a short story may seem like a good idea. But what can appear to be an advantage – brevity – can also be problematic because, by necessity, a short story includes a lot of ideas in a limited space. This means there is less to read, but more is demanded of the reader. Since the writer does not have the space to spell out everything they want to convey, the reader may have to read between the lines and supply what is not stated in order to understand what is going on. This can be challenging and could be more suited to older learners, who have a wider vocabulary, more experience of reading in their L1 and a broader knowledge of the world. Another challenge presented by the short story is that, once a class has worked with one story, the next presents readers with a change of context and, with it, a change of words for describing characters, places and events.

A novel provides a more leisurely introduction to the setting, characters and plot. Once readers become accustomed to these, the familiarity supports their understanding of new developments and language, while key vocabulary related to people and places is often recycled throughout the book. In other words, the meaningful context of the story gives the reader more opportunities to learn new words. Some of this learning will occur incidentally; however, by designing tasks which draw learners' attention to words, teachers also enable explicit learning to take place. The learning process is further supported when learners use the words productively in tasks that involve them in writing and speaking.

Themes

Two of the UK's most prolific and popular children's writers of novels are Jacqueline Wilson and Michael Morpurgo. One reason why their books are loved is that young readers can identify with the themes and the characters which are so vividly depicted. Jacqueline Wilson writes for the 6 to mid-teens age range. Her themes include friendship and conflict, teenage love, same-sex relationships, teenage pregnancy, and family issues such as divorce and its consequences. While most of her main characters are girls, books for the youngest readers in the age range feature both boys and girls. Two examples, based on earlier work by E. Nesbit, are *Four Children and It* (2012) and *The Primrose Railway Children* (2021). Male characters also feature in *Kiss* (2007), which is intended for young teens. In this book, a boy–girl friendship changes as the children reach puberty, and the boy falls in love with another boy.

Written for the 10–14 age range, the relationships at the heart of Michael Morpurgo's work often feature children and animals and are set in exotic locations such as the Indonesian jungle (*Running Wild*; 2009) or South African savannah (*The Butterfly Lion*; 1996). The viewpoint might be that of the child protagonist or the animal. The animal's perspective is used in *Warhorse* (1982), a book which has been adapted for both stage and screen. It tells the story of a farm horse that is taken away to serve in the trenches during the First World War, and his love for Albert, the farmer's son he leaves behind. Morpurgo returns to the same historical context in *Private Peaceful* (2003), which tells of Tommo, a young soldier, and his memories of a happy upbringing and the people he has left at home, contrasting with the horrors of his current existence in the trenches. Though the narrator is an older teen, the target reader is aged 9 to 11. Through their strong characterisation and depiction of setting, action and feelings, both of these books can create empathy in the reader and serve as an introduction to a period of history which might otherwise seem remote.

In addition to his novels, Morpurgo (2014) has adapted a collection of Aesop's fables for the 6 to 9 age range. If learners are already familiar with the tales in their L1, then reading The Hare and the Tortoise, for example, would be possible in English, focusing on both the language and the moral of the tale. For older learners, *Singing for Mrs Pettigrew: A Storymakers' Journey* (2007) is a story collection with a difference. By way of introduction to each story, Morpurgo describes the people, places, events and objects in his own life that have influenced him and on which he has drawn as a writer. Teachers might try to inspire their learners to write by asking them to bring in an object or photograph. The class's joint collection can be used as a resource for individual or collaborative short-story writing. The writing could be preceded by group or class discussion of what the objects or photos are or might represent. As Morpurgo writes in the introduction to this book, 'we all have the seedcorn of stories inside us' (2006:8).

Novels and short stories for different age groups

Very young children are most likely to benefit from picturebooks, graded readers and simple graphic novels before progressing to chapter books. A chapter book is a book for intermediate readers. These books are divided into short chapters, which break up the text and afford the reader time to pause, review and reflect on what they have read before moving on. The books usually contain illustrations to support understanding. Older learners and adults can benefit both from independent reading and from working with longer texts (or collections of shorter texts). Whatever the age or level, the teacher here faces the same question: how do you choose a book to work with?

Finding a book to engage your learners

Some years ago, I carried out a five-week study with 10 to 11-year-olds, based on Roald Dahl's *The Magic Finger*. At the end, the children were asked if they would like to work with another book in English in the future. While they were generally positive towards this (some felt the language was hard), there was a caveat: it would depend on what the book was about. They described the story they had read as 'fun' and 'exciting', and felt that the ending was satisfying. As such, I recommend choosing a book with humour, or one that in some way connects with the interests of your class. The challenge is to find something that everyone can be interested in. Another option is to find a book that links to aspects of the wider curriculum and which could act as a prompt for some project work. After considering the interests of your learners, the wider curriculum and the proficiency level of the class, ask yourself the following questions:

1. Is the title likely to appeal to the learners?
2. Is the cover likely to appeal to the learners?
3. Are there various editions with different covers that you could make use of? (For example, the children can discuss their expectations of the story based on the pictures on the front cover of each version.)
4. Is the story likely to engage the learners?
5. How straightforward is the plot? For example, does it deal with time changes from present to past (that is, are there flashbacks)?
6. Are there a lot of characters to keep track of?
7. Does the first sentence capture attention and is that attention likely to be held at the end of the first paragraph?
8. Is the sentence structure easy enough for them to follow?
9. Are the pages densely packed with long paragraphs or broken up with dialogue?
10. Are there illustrations that could support understanding, provoke interest or be used in tasks?
11. Are there chapters, and if not, how could you break the text up yourself? *The Magic Finger*, for instance, does not have chapters but can be logically divided into sections.
12. What kinds of tasks could you create that target the vocabulary and language skills your learners need to practise?

It is important that the chosen book engages the readers not only because you want them to enjoy it and learn from the associated tasks, but also because they might be encouraged to read on their own. They might be prompted to read other books by the same author or books on a similar theme.

You may not make avid readers out of all your learners, especially when so much else competes for their time these days. But you can introduce them to different worlds, with engaging characters and intriguing plot developments – to worlds that they can experience together. The key to this is finding the book that is right for your class.

Research support for extensive reading

The kind of reading that learners often do in a classroom where their English lessons are based on a coursebook tends to be 'close' (or 'intensive') reading. Texts are short, and the learners read for details in order to answer questions. Tasks like this, which require specific answers, encourage readers to scan for the information, and questions may be answered without a thorough understanding of the content. For example, suppose the text states: *John owned an old blue car*, and the question is: *What colour was John's car?* All the reader has to do is scan for the name 'John' and the word 'car', and then a colour. While scanning is undoubtedly a useful reading strategy, it is not the only one. Moreover, on its own, it is unlikely to result in much engagement with the content.

These shorter texts do offer some opportunities for the development of both reading strategies and language, but there is more support in the research literature for longer texts, including novels and short stories. In his chapter 'Using Literature in ELT', Hall (2016) makes the point that extensive reading, or reading for pleasure, builds confidence. Readers become familiar with the language used to describe setting, characters and plot development; words and phrases may be repeated. This familiarity, which helps the learner to create and sustain visual images of people, place and events, makes it easier for them to process meaning without having to dwell on the linguistic structures and words that convey the meaning. Audiobooks play a similar role with regard to extensive listening (Bland, 2023).

Development of receptive skills

If a learner can grasp the meaning of a text without necessarily understanding every word in it, their confidence in their ability to read a book in the target language is boosted. All major theories of language learning (for example, Lichtman & VanPatten, 2021) acknowledge the importance of input, but there are differing views concerning the incidental learning of vocabulary through reading alone. Critics argue that readers may not notice a word at all if they understand the gist of the text. Others concede that they may notice a word because it disrupts their understanding, but argue that they might just ignore it and hope that the meaning will become clear shortly. This takes us to the question of the level of the reading material.

The problem for the classroom teacher working on one book with a whole class is that, while some learners will know many, most, or all of the words, others will have less knowledge. If the more proficient are to be challenged, and the less proficient supported, much depends on the tasks that the teacher creates around the book. I would like to give some examples of what I mean from my study using *The Magic Finger*, which I first mentioned in Chapter 1. One aim of the study was to find out what the learners enjoyed, or not, about working with a children's novel in their English lessons; they had not done this before. Another was to investigate to what extent they could learn vocabulary from the book without being taught explicitly, but through meeting it in a range of tasks that they worked on. All the teaching was carried out by the class teachers; my role in the classroom was to observe and make notes.

During the study period, the children worked with a jigsaw of a part of the story – putting in order pieces of the text written on slips of paper. In a task of this kind, the more proficient can be given a longer extract, and therefore more slips of paper to read, digest and organise. Those who need more support can be told which lines come first and which last, in order to provide a framework. Another alternative is to let the less proficient work with a shorter extract, and here, too, you might give them the beginning and end of the extract.

In a task which required the learners (in pairs) to predict what would happen when the ducks take over the family's house, the learners drew a picture and wrote a sentence. Here, the more proficient can be asked to write more than one connected sentence to develop this part of the story; the less proficient might draw and label their picture without having to construct a sentence.

The Magic Finger was chosen for the study for the following reasons:

- It is by a major author. (Dahl's work was already known to many of the children in their first language, or through film, and the teachers and I thought it could be interesting for them to read his work in English.)
- It is short (18 pages), with a simple plot and a limited number of characters.
- It is humorous and likely to appeal to boys and girls. (Research has found that, while boys and girls often prefer different things, humour appeals to both.)
- It contains both everyday vocabulary and less common words.
- There are full-colour illustrations (at least, in the version we used). This made the text visually appealing and also allowed colour details to be exploited when the children described what they saw in a picture, for instance.

The day before the study began, the learners were tested on 20 keywords, chosen as being useful in everyday English and/or helpful in supporting understanding of the story. The table below contains 21 words. That is because the word *farm* (number 14) was used as an example by the teachers when they demonstrated the task to the learners. The task involved matching a picture with each word, by writing the respective word's number under each picture. Before they did the test, the teachers made sure that the children understood what the pictures represented in L1.

1. nest	8. funny	15. lake
2. tiny	9. soil	16. wet
3. dove	10. woods	17. biscuit
4. smash	11. hunting	18. sticks
5. gate	12. noise	19. star
6. sunshine	13. window	20. deer
7. play	14. farm	21. slug

During the study – three lessons of 40–50 minutes per week over the five-week period – the learners (1) heard the words as the teacher read from the book, (2) read them when they worked with parts of the text themselves, and (3) encountered them in different tasks, both receptively and productively, but did not learn them for homework. On the final day of the study, they did the same test, and again two weeks later, during which time they had not worked with the book.

Of the 23 children who completed all three tests, most knew at least ten words at the beginning. Three knew all 20. Of these, one was a bilingual speaker of Swedish and English, and the other two were keen gamers, which may have had an influence as gaming is said to boost learners' vocabulary resources. The gains seen in the second test ranged in number from one word to ten, with most of the children scoring five more words. Almost all the children maintained their score on being tested a third time two weeks later, during which time they had not worked with the words. It seems, then, that while explicit learning of vocabulary is often said to be more efficient than incidental learning, there is much teachers can do to create ways for readers to meet and notice words themselves.

Development of productive skills

A vocabulary test of the kind described above tells us whether or not the learners know what a word means. To gain an insight into how well they could use the words, I gave the children a picture of ducks on a lake and asked them to write a story or descriptive text around it. They did this before starting the study and again at the end, using the same picture. The second time they did it, they were encouraged to use any words they had learnt from the story *The Magic Finger*.

The second texts the children produced were mostly no longer than the first ones. One reason for this was that the children did not seem motivated to write. They said this was because they had already written about this picture. However, when prompted to write another kind of text (for example, a story if they had written a description before), most managed to produce more text. This acted as a useful reminder that it really does not matter how much your learners know if they are not motivated to show it!

Nevertheless, a comparison of the 'before' and 'after' texts was informative with regard to the children's vocabulary development. For example, a number of children used the L1 word for 'duck' in the first text but used the English word in the second. Another learner had not known the word 'tiny' on the first test but knew it on the second and used it in her second text.

No grammar was taught during the study period and no attention was paid to the verb forms in the text. The main structures in the book are the simple and past continuous, with instances of present and past perfect, *will* for future reference, and the passive voice. The children's texts – written both before and after the reading of the book – were of interest as a window into what the children knew or were in the process of learning. For example, the third person s had been taught in their previous English lessons, based on their coursebook. While some learners displayed full control, for others, control was partial. In the two consecutive sentences, 'The man have hair. He lives in a house', the learner uses the correct verb form in the second sentence – third person s – but not the first.

The learners' writing both before and after the study also displayed attempts to use structures that they had not yet learnt in English lessons: 'I can se that the ducks has swimd in the lake bicus it is tiny bubbles'. The present perfect had not been taught, nor had the class worked with subordinate clauses. A further example is an attempt at the passive voice: 'The family eats up of a fox' (= The family is eaten up by a fox). The learner may have picked up a structure incidentally while working with the book, or they may have been aware of it already. The important thing about reading stories is that where the children are interested in the text and motivated to work on tasks which allow them to make full use of their linguistic repertoire, they are likely to show the teacher (and themselves) what they know and can do in English.

Telling the story

Some children enjoy listening to the teacher read the story to them; others prefer to read for themselves. This highlights the importance of varying the way you work with the story and the kinds of tasks you create. One thing I would recommend is that you do not ask the children to listen for too long; pause and ask questions about what they think is going to happen. This gives everyone some breathing space to absorb what they are hearing and to reflect. It is also a way of drawing them into events as they unfold.

Extended writing

Along with the benefits of extended reading in the classroom, there are also advantages to having your learners write their own longer pieces of text. As we saw earlier with the children's texts about the ducks, if they write about a topic similar to the one they have read about or listened to, they can be encouraged to use some of the words they have met, worked with and noted in their reading. For instance, Jacqueline Wilson's *Best Friends* (2008) tells the story of two friends who are parted by a great distance, something that some young learners may have experienced. Learners could be asked to write a letter from one friend to the other, bringing in details from the book about what is happening in their (character's) life. As an extension, learners could create and describe an imaginary friend, complete with drawings and details of family background and daily life.

Similarly, after reading *The Magic Finger*, the children could write a narrative text beginning, 'One day I woke up and found I had a magic finger. I am going to tell you about my day.' This prompts the use of the past tense and will require adverbials such as *then, next, in the afternoon, before I went to bed*, and so on. For lower-proficiency learners, an alternative to continuous prose is to list what they did or would do with their magic finger. Alternatively, the learners could choose another superpower and describe how they would use it. Again, lower-proficiency learners might make a list rather than write in continuous prose.

A stimulus for extended writing

There are a number of ways of providing a stimulus to write. I mentioned one earlier in connection with Michael Morpurgo's short stories – that learners bring in items which have a personal meaning for them. Another stimulus to write can be an event in a story, perhaps one that draws on a learner's own experiences and emotions.

Images and music are also forms of stimulus which can lead to learners creating their own story. Bermayo and Guillén conducted a project (described in Bland & Lütge, 2013) that involved both younger and older primary learners in Spain producing their own content. Their work began with brainstorming and creating individual characters. The stimulus for this was a piece of music, and the authors highlight the importance of both music and art for sparking the imagination. These are important as starting points because everyone can relate to them, regardless of proficiency. From here, the learners worked in groups, chose one of the characters that had been created and came up with a story. To do this, they made flow charts, drawings, lists of words and skeleton notes, which they then edited to produce the finished product. The same procedure could be used to create a sequel or prequel for a book that the class has worked with.

In a more extensive writing project than the Spanish one described above, Andrew Wright worked with Austrian 11 to 12-year-olds (described in Bland & Lütge, 2013). In his project, the children created their own short books, working through stages of researching, drafting, editing, illustrating and producing a finished small book. Wright makes the point that words are not solo instruments, i.e. they rarely occur on their own, and yet a very common type of classroom vocabulary task (and test) is one in which the teacher gives the learners either the L1 or L2 form of a word, and they have to supply the translation. The title of Wright's chapter is *Stories as symphonies*, a striking way of describing a story. Just like musical notes in a symphony, words come together to create a unique meaning in a story. This is something that young learners should be aware of and proud of in their writing work. Again, Wright's project was about creating stories with children rather than working with a specific book, but the procedure can be applied to working with an existing story. For instance, take *Cinderboy*, mentioned in Chapter 4. The learners might create a character who has a dream but faces opposition. The character's life takes a turn for the better when someone (the fairy godmother figure) gives a helping hand, and in the end the character's dreams come true. Having worked with *Cinderboy*, a teacher I knew wrote about her own character, Swimerella, who wanted to be an Olympic swimmer. The teacher used her story as a model for the children (aged 12) to create their own stories in the way that Andrew Wright's learners had, resulting in small, laminated books that were first put on display in the classroom for everyone to read, and which the writers then took home.

Let us now go on to look at some of the practical ways in which you can review the content of a novel or short story with your learners. The first two tasks deal with factual content, the others with vocabulary. They require little preparation on the part of the teacher; some lend themselves to getting the learners involved in the preparation stage. They are suitable for all age groups and can be used both while reading the book and afterwards. In addition, they can be adapted to take up around ten minutes of lesson time to be used as warm-up or closure tasks.

Practical applications

The True/False Circle

This activity requires learners to listen carefully and compare the accuracy of what they hear with what they know of the story. You do need quite a bit of space for this.

Procedure:

1. Divide the learners into small groups and ask each group to stand in a small circle.
2. Tell them they will hear statements based on the book. If the statement is correct, they take one step to the right (i.e. anticlockwise); if it is incorrect, they take one step to the left (i.e. clockwise). If they do not know the answer, they step back. For the youngest learners, this is enough.
3. For older learners, or to add an extra challenge, you could say that if they think the answer is not in the story, they step forward. For example, if working with *The Magic Finger*, a statement could be: 'The Gregg family will never be cruel to animals again'. The likely response to this is that it is true, based on the fact that the family was turned into ducks, but on the other hand, they were once keen hunters, so some learners may have their doubts. The undecided learners could step forward here. Where

some step to the right and others step forward, there is an opportunity to discuss the different views.

The first time you work with this, demonstrate the steps with a piece of information that is very familiar so the class get the idea of what they have to do. Taking the decision to move clockwise or anticlockwise can be a challenge in itself without the additional possibility of stepping back or forward. One possible issue with this task is that those who do not know the answer can simply follow the others, rather than show they do not know by stepping back. On the other hand, it does allow them to 'save face' – and they now have a chance to learn.

The main aim of this task is for the teacher to see if there are any misunderstandings regarding the events in the story. If you say, for example, in relation to *The Magic Finger*, that the Gregg family develop wings (which is correct), you will expect the learners to move to the right. If some move to the left and bump into each other, the misunderstanding can be sorted out on the spot. The children might find the unexpected collision funny, thereby reducing any anxiety about getting the answer wrong. The correct answer may be more easily remembered too. One more benefit of this task is that it gets the learners out of their seats and moving. With the appropriate classroom atmosphere, it can be fun.

Variation:

The children remain at their desks. If the statement is correct, they put their hands on their heads, or give the thumbs-up; if it is incorrect, they place their hands on the desk or give the thumbs down. They can indicate uncertainty by folding their arms or by pointing their thumb inwards. This variation is suitable for the youngest children, who may find it hard to remember which way they are supposed to be moving. In addition, you can easily see what their responses are from the front of the class.

Two True, One False

Preparation: This works best when the class has finished reading a book. In advance of the lesson, the learners write three statements about the story or characters. Two of them should be correct, and one false. This draws on their knowledge of the plot, characters and setting; it also helps them to recall words from the book and encourages them to construct correct sentences in English.

Procedure:

1. Arrange the learners in groups of three, facing each other.
2. One person stands up and reads out their three statements.
3. The other two agree on which statement is false. If they answer correctly, the learner who is standing gives them a clap. If they get it wrong, they clap the speaker.
4. The speaker sits down, and the next one stands to read out their statements.

This continues until all three have read out their statements and received a response. Asking the children to speak in front of their peers puts them in the spotlight, so this is a good way of easing them into speaking in front of others. It also shows you when the class has finished, as everyone is sitting. As for clapping, this reinforces the success of the learners, either as speakers or listeners.

Figure 5.1 shows a child's work from The Magic Finger study:

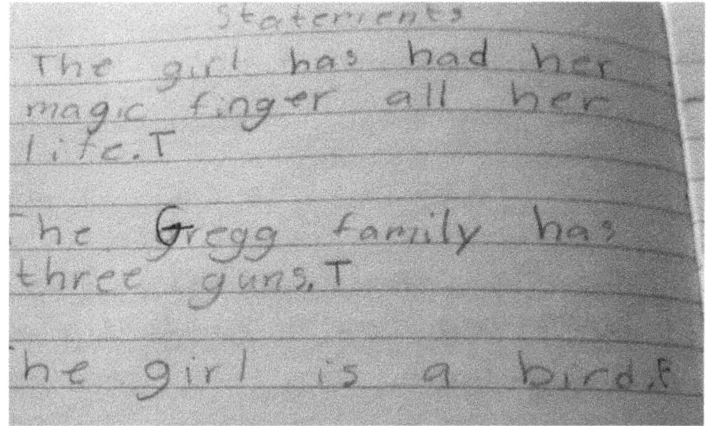

Figure 5.1: Two true statements and one false

The following review tasks deal with words from a book. Again, it can be used as you work through the story or at the end.

Words on the Board

This activity encourages learners to practise reading and understanding a text sufficiently well to be able to match a word on the page with one of 10 to 15 on the whiteboard.

Preparation:

1. Select a page from the book for each pair of learners in the class.
2. From each of these pages, choose a word that you think is important for the children to know, making sure (if possible) that it appears on only one of the pages.

Procedure:

1. Put the learners into pairs. Give each pair a page from the book.
2. Write the L1 forms of the words you have chosen on the whiteboard.
3. Tell the children that they have to find the L2 word for one of them on the page they have been given.
4. When they find the matching word, they come to the board and write it next to the L1 word in a different colour.

The difference between this task and a traditional way of checking vocabulary, where the teacher provides the L1 form and the learners provide the L2, is that success here does not depend on whether or not they can recall the word, but whether they can recognise it in context. This is easier, but at the same time more challenging since they have to read the text. Those who know what the L1 words are in English are likely to apply a scanning technique; the less proficient are likely to read the text more closely.

Creating pairs, threes or fours based on vocabulary

This is one way of creating pairs or groups to work together in a lesson or series of lessons.

Preparation for pairs:

Make cards with the L1 and L2 forms of a word.

Preparation for threes/fours:

Add a card which has a picture of the word. This works well with concrete items, and as such can be used with the youngest learners. For a group of four, add a definition of the word.

Procedure: Give each child a card. Explain that they have to find their partner (or the rest of their group, if you are working with threes or fours). They either show each other their word/picture/definition, or say it, depending on whether you want them to focus on the written or the spoken form of the word.

Extension:

The learners make the sets of cards themselves. Give pairs of learners an L2 word. They check they know the L1 equivalent, write the word on a card, draw a representation and write the definition. This means they have to really think about their words, which in turn supports learning. Making sets of cards can be an ongoing activity in class for gradually building up a lexical resource. The cards can be used for making pairs and groups, as described above, but they can also act as stimuli for creating oral or written stories. Additionally, the definitions can be used as described in the next task.

Pass the Pencil

This game involves listening to a definition and deciding which word is being defined.

Preparation: In pairs, or individually, learners write a definition of a word that the class has met in the book and which has previously been included as homework. As with *Two True, One False*, have them do this in an earlier lesson, and tell them the class will be working with their definitions. Collect the definitions.

Procedure:

Before getting started with the game, do a trial run so the children understand what they have to do.

1. Arrange the children in groups of four, preferably around a desk so they can see each other.
2. Put one piece of paper and one pencil between them on the desk.
3. Play some music. As the music plays, the children pass the pencil around the group.
4. When the music stops, they stop passing the pencil.
5. Read out one of the definitions. The group agree on which word is being defined, and the child holding the pencil writes the word down. Adding

a time limit here increases the challenge and encourages the learners to think quickly and collaborate.

6. The music starts, and they start passing the pencil around again. The game continues until all the definitions have been read out, or until you feel it's a good time to stop. Six to eight is a good number, so you might not use all the definitions in one game.
7. Go through the answers with the class.

Examples of definitions that learners wrote during *The Magic Finger* study include: 1) 'This thing has wings and feathers' (Answer: a bird); 2) 'You can hit with it' (Answer: a hammer); 3) 'I look up and see that it is blue' (Answer: the sky). Note that in a low-proficiency class, you can provide a list of possible words on the whiteboard before you start the game. These words could be the target L2 words (i.e. the answers), or they could be the L1 translations, pushing learners to think a little harder. You can increase the challenge by including in the list one or two distractors (i.e. extra words that are not in the book).

This is a popular way to work with words and concepts, and it is suitable for learners of all ages. If they cannot write a whole sentence in L2, perhaps they can do this in L1, and if they cannot manage a whole sentence, then the L1 word is enough. What always strikes me is the laughter when the pencil stops. It is fun, and when it is fun, the pressure is off, and the learners benefit from it.

The Hungry Crocodile

This comes from Carol Read's (2007) *500 Activities for the Primary Classroom*. It is a version of the more familiar Hangman and practises L2 letter names and spelling. The teacher chooses a word and for each letter writes a dash on the whiteboard. In this game, there is a man who wants to cross a river. Every time the learners fail to suggest a correct letter for the word, he is taken one step closer to the jaws of the crocodile, as shown in Figure 5.2. Letters which have been suggested but not used are written on the whiteboard, as seen on the left of the picture.

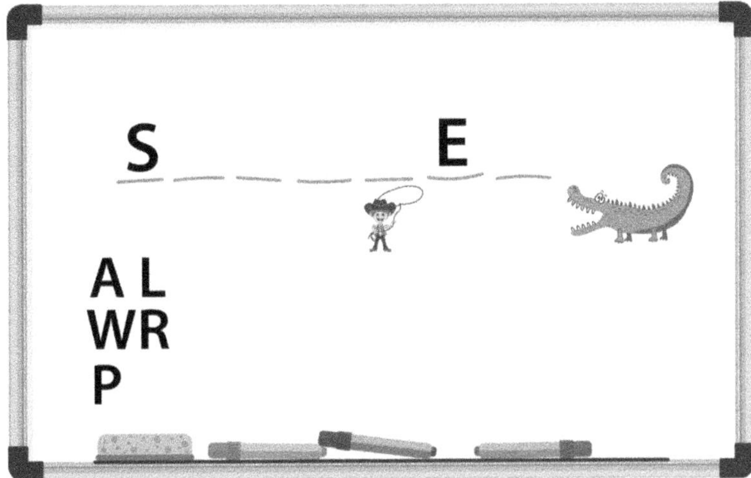

Figure 5.2: The Hungry Crocodile

One potential issue with this game, as with Hangman, is that children might actually enjoy seeing the man meet an unhappy end and deliberately guess wrongly. A possible solution for this is to turn the game into an ongoing contest between the class and you. If they save the man, they score a point; if they do not, you score the point. Another concern that teachers have is that the learners are not equally involved: some see immediately which letters are needed, while others need more time. To mitigate this, try creating small teams and ensuring the team members agree on each suggestion. Remember, though, that there is nothing wrong with some learners being quiet sometimes. Participation is not only about being visibly active, it is also about being interested and mentally engaged. In these conditions, learning can occur.

Moving from word-based games to text-based games

Both *Pass the Pencil* and *The Hungry Crocodile* focus on the meaning of individual words. This might be enough for the youngest learners. To adapt the games so that older or more advanced learners practise producing longer pieces of text, ask them to use some of these keywords to write a summary of the story, for example, or a description of a character or place. To introduce a game-type aspect to the task, ask learners to include something untrue in their summary or description. Not everyone has to falsify details as this could be hard for some. When they have finished, display the texts around the classroom. Everyone reads them and decides which ones have an incorrect detail in them, and what it is. Go through their answers, asking each writer to confirm whether the details are correct or not.

Where there is an element of uncertainty, as here, there is the potential for curiosity – a reason to read more attentively, and to think. The benefits are that everyone's text becomes of interest, is read carefully, and the content of the book is reviewed. If the children work in pairs, they provide peer support; where they do not agree, more attention may be paid to the language, regardless of whether some or all their discussion is in L1.

Another task that involves producing longer stretches of text involves learners writing a summary or description and removing one or two of the keywords. This creates a gapped text. This time, their classmates have to replace the words that have been removed. To support them, you could create a list of all the missing words from the texts, perhaps with one or two extras to make it a little more challenging.

Professional development

Questions for reflection

- Think of a class that you would like to work on a novel with. Go through the 'Finding a book' checklist on page 74. Are there any other criteria you think are important when choosing a book?
- What do you see as the challenges for choosing and using a book that is suitable for your class? How would you overcome these issues??

Things to try

- Choose a book and carry out a study similar to the one based on *The Magic Finger*, described in this chapter. Test your learners on the core vocabulary before you start, immediately after you've finished working with the book, and again two weeks later. Compare the results. If the majority of your class manage to remember most of the words, ask them why they think this was the case.
- Think of a game that you have played in your first language that could be adapted to help learners review the content or the language of a novel. Try it out. Then share your experience with another teacher.

Further reading

Ahlquist, S. (2020). Embedding language-development tasks in lessons based on The Magic Finger in the primary classroom. *Children's Literature in English Language Education, CLELE*, 8(2): 64–85.

Bland, J., & Lütge, C. (Eds.) (2013). *Children's literature in second language education*. London: Bloomsbury.

Read, C. (2007). *500 Activities for the Primary Classroom*. Oxford: Macmillan.

6. Using the Storyline approach

The Storyline approach (often referred to simply as 'Storyline') originated in Scotland in the 1960s in response to a requirement for interdisciplinary teaching in primary schools (Bell & Harkness, 2006). It involves bringing together content from different curriculum areas in the framework of a story, in which the pupils, working in small groups, take on the roles of characters. The story unfolds (typically over four to six weeks) as the learners work on tasks related to 'Key Questions'. These are open questions which structure the story, introduce events of various kinds, and connect the tasks to a subject syllabus or to wider curriculum content. Texts and drawings produced by the pupils are displayed on a free-standing frieze, or on the walls of the classroom. Today, Storyline is used in many parts of the world, at all levels of the education system, and in both L1 and L2 contexts. In the L2 classroom, the use of language in a variety of meaningful tasks brings the language to life and supports the development of knowledge and skills.

Even though Storyline has been around since the 1960s, and has certainly gained traction in language education, there is very little research relating to the approach itself. Theoretical support can, however, be found in the learning theories of both Piaget and Vygotsky. For Piaget, learning development occurs through a child's interaction with the physical environment and engagement with tasks. Through that engagement, the child actively constructs their knowledge based on what they already know. In Storyline, children create the story world together, working on practical and language-based tasks, building up a visual representation of place, people and happenings. Through tasks which draw the learner's attention to the frieze on which the story is displayed, and through other tasks which develop the story, the teacher can promote vocabulary development and integrate meaningful ways to practise various aspects of the spoken and written language.

For Vygotsky, interaction with other people is an important source of learning, and learning development is seen best when the learner is working with a more capable other. This is an important consideration for teachers deciding how to group their learners, especially so in Storyline, where the story is developed over a number of weeks with learners working in the same group throughout. Because of the nature of the work – both practical and language-based – a group will ideally consist of learners with a range of skills. For example, a low-proficiency learner may have artistic skills that are useful to the group. For each individual, being able to make a valuable contribution is an important factor in providing motivation for them to engage with the task.

Storyline in second language education

Storyline takes a sociocultural, communicative approach similar to task-based teaching and learning. When the approach is applied to a language learning context, learners learn the language by using it to complete tasks, as well as when they take on the roles of characters in a story. The stories can be created from scratch and set, for example, on a farm, in a wildlife park, at a circus, hotel, airport, school or even in the planetary system. The characters can be humans, aliens or, especially in the younger learner classroom, animals. The learners create and introduce their characters using a drawing or a model; then they write about the character. Other genres of writing (e.g. letters, instructions, posters and invitations) or speaking (e.g. role play, discussion and songs) can be practised and developed in relation to the topic. As well as using the approach to create an imagined world from scratch, teachers can choose to create a Storyline based on an existing book.

How Storyline works in practice

Some years ago, I carried out a five-week study with a class of children aged 11–13 (Ahlquist, 2013). The aim was to investigate what aspects of Storyline the children liked more, or less, how they thought they learnt through the approach, and how the two teachers of the class saw learning develop over the five-week period. The story the children worked with was not based on an existing story, so they had to come up with characters and create a setting, speaking and writing in role. The study process was as follows:

Study purpose established: to investigate the popularity of aspects of Storyline, language development and learners' own views of how and what they learn through Storyline; Storyline outline, Key Questions and tasks planned with teachers; materials prepared.

↓

Learners grouped by teachers.

↓

Learners rate their own proficiency in English based on a scale for each of speaking, listening, reading and writing.

↓

Storyline begins; learners complete a weekly journal on likes/dislikes and learning. Observation notes made, also video recording and photos.

↓

Storyline ends; learners complete a questionnaire about their likes and dislikes of tasks; they rate their proficiency again; interviews with teachers and learners conducted.

↓

Data analysis carried out in relation to the research questions; findings synthesised; conclusions reached.

The Storyline was about families living in a street in a fictitious English town. It was intended to consolidate the grammar and vocabulary that the children already knew and to introduce the vocabulary of sustainability, which they had been working with in L1. The children created families, and drew and wrote about their houses. Events in the story included the arrival of a new family in the street, taking part in a project to live more sustainably, experiencing a spate of burglaries and, because Storylines generally end with a celebration, organising a street party.

The children's questionnaire and interview responses demonstrated that they had enjoyed the variety of tasks and the different ways in which they had used English. The less proficient learners reported that they found they could easily get help from their groupmates, and many enjoyed using their imagination to create, draw and act as their characters. Children often used the word 'fun' to describe the experience, noting that when something is fun, you make more effort and then you learn more. Learning benefits included more willingness to speak English in class, the ability to produce longer and more complex written texts, the acquisition of new words, a better understanding of how question words are used and an improved grasp of word order.

Storyline based on existing stories

Although the story in my study was created from scratch, it is possible to use similar tasks, such as creating characters, setting a scene and dialogues when working with published children's fiction aimed at all levels and age groups.

Younger primary-age learners

One story that is suitable for L2 learners in the early stages of learning English is *The Lighthouse Keeper's Lunch* (Ronda and David Armitage), first published in 1977. The L1 target age range is 3 to 6. The story is about a lighthouse keeper who lives with his wife in a small cottage on a cliff. Every day, he rows out to the lighthouse on a rock in the sea. At lunchtime, his wife sends food in a basket down a wire from the cottage to the lighthouse. Working in groups, the learners create parts of the setting (cliffs, cottage, sea, rock, lighthouse, and characters), and place these appropriately on the frieze.

The lunches are briefly described in the text, and from these descriptions each group can be responsible for drawing and labelling the items for each basket. They might also include other items in the baskets, justifying why the lighthouse keeper would like these. Once a wire has been added to the frieze, linking the cottage and lighthouse, the food baskets for different days can be placed there. The story is about how the lighthouse keeper and his wife try to stop seagulls from stealing the food from the baskets. There are opportunities for speculation at various stages, for example, what the learners think the lighthouse keeper will do next, and whether that will stop the seagulls. The drawings on the frieze (or classroom walls) can be labelled; short texts can be written to describe the characters, the setting and the events. Dialogues can be predicted (such as between the man and wife) and compared with what is said in the book. Where there is no dialogue, this can be imagined. For example, when the seagulls steal sandwiches only to find they are filled with mustard, children can be encouraged to think about what they might say to each other. Once the story is finished, the learners can use the frieze to retell the events, either by speaking or in writing. Finally, the teacher can use the texts and images displayed there to create a quiz. The learners answer the questions by looking carefully at the visual display.

Older primary-age learners

A story that I've found works well with 11 to 12-year-olds is Roald Dahl's *Fantastic Mr Fox*, where L2 development can be promoted by combining Storyline with the existing story. The plot of the book is straightforward: three farmers attempt to kill the fox that has been stealing from them to feed its family. The first two chapters introduce the characters. The text that describes them is very short. Storyline can be built up around a reading of this text. This can be done by dividing the class into four and assigning each group a task. The groups can be given either one of the farmers or the fox to work on for Key Question 1: Who are the characters?

Give the groups a number of tasks to complete between them and a stated time in which to do so, such as drawing the character and their imagined home, writing about the character, and describing a typical day. Ask the learners to use their imagination and to read between the lines. Monitor and give assistance where required. Then ask the groups to take turns presenting their character to the class. You can display their work around the classroom or on your Learning Management System (LMS), if you have one.

Figure 6. 1 shows an example of what a learner might imagine a day in the life of Mr Fox would be like.

You can then move on to the second chapter, in which the farmers have a plan to kill the fox. The learners work in their groups again; ask them to come up with an idea for what the plan could be. This is the second Key Question: What do you think the farmers are going to do? Give each member of the group one part of the text in which the plan unfolds. Tell them to draw a picture, based on their text. Then get them to look at each other's pictures and to try to work out a sequence of events. Again, go around monitoring and help with language where necessary. Then ask the learners to write a short text to accompany each picture (Figure 6.2).

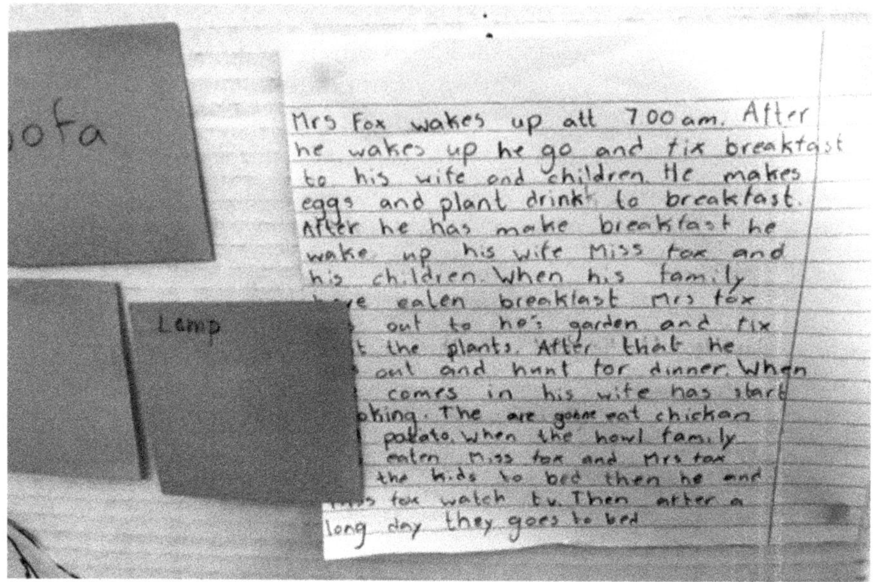

Figure 6.1: A day in the life of Mr Fox

Figure 6.2: Sequence of events based on reading

Lastly, explain or read to the class what actually happens. (Mr Fox is shot, but not seriously injured.)

At this point, display a picture of a shovel on the whiteboard and read the book as far as the words: 'the most frightening sound a fox can hear'. Encourage the class to discuss what this could be. (Answer: the farmers are digging.) Write on the whiteboard Key Question 3: How do you think Mr Fox tries to save his family? Put the class in their groups and ask them to create a dialogue between the members of the fox family about what they should do. You could say that each member of the group should create at least two lines of dialogue. Monitor, as before, giving assistance where needed. Then get the groups to take turns acting out their dialogues. Read Chapter 4, which deals with this part of the story.

The danger continues. In Chapter 5, the farmers decide to dig the fox family out with their tractors. Before you read the chapter to the class, show a picture from the book (people staring into an enormous crater caused by the farmers using their tractors) and get the children to speculate individually as to what has happened. They write their ideas in their notebooks. They can then compare their thoughts with those of their groupmates.

As the story moves on, the farmers camp out, waiting for the fox to appear, and decide to use all their workers to help them. Read Chapter 8 to the class and ask them to listen for how many workers each farmer has. You then ask them to add up the total, and each group tells you what their answer is.

The next part of the story deals with the way in which Mr Fox tunnels into a farmer's storehouse to get food for his family. Before you read this to the class, have the learners work in groups. Give them each one of the pictures from this part of the story. They do not look at each other's pictures. They should describe their picture to the group, listen to each other and decide which order the pictures should go in. They can check this order as you read Chapter 10 to them, showing the pictures.

Task your learners to read individually about either a farmer's storehouse or cider cellar, drawing a picture based on the description. They then give instructions to a classmate who has drawn the other place on how to draw this. Figure 6.3 shows an example of this.

Figure 6.3: Read, draw and describe to a partner

The book also offers an opportunity to discuss moral issues in a way that the children can relate to. For instance, while Mr Fox is taking food through the tunnel, he meets Badger, who questions whether the fox has any right to this food. Fox also meets Rat, who tells him to leave the food alone because he got there first and so it belongs to him. In both cases, the discussion might start with the learners individually writing Mr Fox's verbal responses to Badger and to Rat in their notebooks. They can compare what they have each written in the group and sum up their views. This can then lead into a class discussion, giving everyone the opportunity to first think, write their thoughts and tell these to the group. In other words, every learner has an equal chance of being involved than is often the case with group discussion.

Storyline projects usually end with some kind of celebration to draw the work to a close. This Storyline could end with a party to which other animals are invited to share the food that Mr Fox has taken from the farmers. The children might design invitations, write a speech for Mr Fox to deliver, come up with a menu, or create games based on the vocabulary of the book. In a longer piece of work, they might write the next instalment – what will the farmers do now?

You will find that, through using Storyline, your learners will improve their English communication skills and knowledge. My study (Ahlquist, 2021), first mentioned in Chapter 1, highlighted children using idiomatic language and structures they had not yet worked with at school in their texts, in addition to the vocabulary from the book, such as 'We need to get the heck out of here'; 'They took a deep breth'; 'The sun had started to go down'; 'Mr fox was late cuz he was arguing with mr mouse'; 'If you don't let me, I will eat you'. Their texts also revealed a level of uncertainty about newer language the children had been introduced to, for instance: 'The small fox give she a bird'; '… he's favourite food'; 'Are we going to eat they?' This use of language can be helpful in showing you where your learners are in their language development and can demonstrate where remedial or recycling work is required.

You may also find that there will be variation in the kinds of tasks which are popular: some children will prefer the writing and others the speaking. Many of the learners in my study commented that they noticed their speaking ability improved through the different tasks; they also liked the element of uncertainty involved in having to predict what was likely to happen next, i.e. a form of gamification. What is particularly interesting is that the popularity of unpredictability is something that comes up time and time again in my Storyline work.

One of my research questions in the *Fantastic Mr Fox* study related to how helpful the learners found a) the pictures in the book and b) drawing tasks. Interestingly, in each case about half the pupils answered that these were helpful, but others did not know. To help your learners understand the importance of images, draw their attention to the pictures in a book. Ask how a picture might help if they don't understand something in the text. Ask them if seeing or hearing a word is easier to remember if they look at a picture at the same time. This is a hard one for children to answer, so you might want to try it out in your classroom, showing pictures of some new words but not of others. It could be useful for both you and the class to see what difference the pictures might make for some learners. Also, talk to them about the ways in which drawing can help them to learn. Ask if they find it easier to remember words if they have drawn a picture which uses these words. Does it help them to remember the story if they look at the things they have drawn?

Even though some of the children were uncertain about the helpfulness of visuals, I remember a day when the teacher wanted to check their understanding of the story so far. She did this using 'true or false'. The statement was: 'Farmer Bunce has got black hair'. At this, every head in the room swivelled to look – or try to look – at the frieze at the back of the room, where there were drawings of the farmers (shown in Figure 6.4).

Figure 6.4: The frieze created for Fantastic Mr Fox

Beyond language development, the Storyline approach involves opportunities for collaboration, communication, creativity, development of information and technology skills, metacognition, problem-solving and critical thinking. These are just some of the skills that bodies such as the OECD (Organization for Economic Cooperation and Development) consider essential for life in the 21st century and are therefore invaluable components of young learners' education.

Older learners

For older learners, try using the book *Gone*, by Michael Grant (2014), which tells the story of a small community in California. One morning, at the stroke of 10 o'clock, everyone over the age of 15 disappears. With no adults around, the teenagers have to make their community function, faced with an existential threat from the pupils at another school. The youngsters in this book have various superpowers to help them do this.

Although the book itself is quite long, you can select sections of the story for your Storyline, which might only be done for an hour each week, over a four- to six-week period. By making the characters in the story a little younger, I think the Storyline I am going to outline would appeal to your older primary learners too. The most important element of Storyline is group work, so map out your aims, the Key Questions which structure the story, and the tasks which will be worked on 1) as a group and 2) individually, so that you have a balance. Individual work is important for assessment purposes. Try to have contingency plans for each stage because no matter how well you think the stages out, due to Storyline's unpredictable nature, things can go wrong; prompts or extra guidance can help get the Storyline back on track.

You may want to illustrate the story by starting the Storyline off in an unconventional way, such as not being in the room: in a study I carried out some years ago, the teachers hid in a cupboard in the hall, and had cameras rigged up in each of their classrooms so they could see what the learners did when there was no teacher in charge. Some of the learners went into the corridor, messing about; some stayed at their desks, took out their phones and directed their attention to these; others chatted; a few went up to the teacher's desk to see if there were any instructions. On the desk were an envelope and a pile of papers. The papers included copies of the introduction, in which the clock strikes ten, the adults disappear and panic breaks out. Another paper had instructions on it asking the learners to read the extract and compare the characters' behaviour with the way they had reacted when the teachers were not present. It got the learners' attention, and in the follow-up discussion with the teachers (when they returned to their respective classrooms), the learners made it clear that they were very aware that the chaotic response had been similar, the difference being that there was no sense of panic.

The same teachers also experimented with putting the learners in their three classes together and dividing them up according to proficiency.

Normally they grouped their learners in mixed proficiency groups, but this time they wanted to see how the learners would respond to working with those of a similar language level. Again, this serves to depart from the norm and to echo the apparent anarchy in the book – something you could try if there are other classes of the same level in your school taking place at the same time, and willing fellow teachers, of course.

Whether you try the unconventional start or not, use the overview or introduction of the story to get your learners to work on their own to create their individual characters and superpowers, and write texts describing them. Then place the learners in groups, based on the kinds of superpower they have chosen, and ask them to come up with the qualities of a good leader. Next, instruct the class that they are going to have a leadership contest. To do the contest, each group has to write and then record a speech, answering why they should be the leader. Tell them they can embellish their recordings with extra sound or images if they wish. Then play the speeches in class and invite the learners to vote on the winner (choose whether they can vote for their own or not). Count up the votes and determine the winner. At the end, encourage the class to evaluate what 'persuaded' them. For example, was it the words or the performance that got their vote? Put the ideas on the board, then move into a discussion about the qualities of an effective speech.

The next part of the Storyline is getting the class to identify other functions of society from the story, such as meeting basic needs and preserving order. Ask each group to present their individual superpowers, then get the chosen leader group to allocate the functions of society that have been identified to the groups with the most appropriate superpowers. To do this, you will need to choose your Key Questions for the Storyline carefully – it is not just about creating a place and people, it is also about the things that happen, both good and less good. The happenings also bring in the need for different genres and new vocabulary so you will need to monitor and give language assistance where necessary.

One of the problems that the community faced in the Storyline (not actually in the book) was a water shortage. In such cases, you may find your learners will draw on other real-life or learning experiences to complete the tasks. As an example, one group in the study resolved the water shortage by drawing on material they had recently worked with in their chemistry lessons and applying it to the problem. This was something that happened naturally –

they had not been asked to do it. In other words, using a Storyline at this level illustrates the fact that carefully considered tasks can cover more extensive amounts of curriculum content, not just English. At the end, ask each group to present their ideas to the class, and then invite discussion around the feasibility of the ideas.

The last part of the Storyline can deal with what happens next to the newly formed student community, and how the story will end. You could do the following:

- Read out an extract from later on in the book and invite the class to speculate on what has happened. They write their ideas in their notebooks.
- Write a synopsis from different sections of the book on different pieces of paper and hand them out to the groups. Get the learners to work together to decide which order the different synopses go in. Then ask them to present their ideas to the other groups, explaining why they chose the order they did.
- Task your learners to write from their character's point of view about how they were feeling during a particular scene – you can ask the learners to select a particular one themselves. Then get them to compare experiences to see if they have described similar feelings to anyone else.
- Ask the groups to suggest no more than five rules which should govern behaviour in the new community.

When the Storyline draws to a close, gather feedback from the participants. You may find some learners enjoy working with the other classes and the opportunity to work with new people – something that may be important to them as it echoes real life. Others may say they prefer working with their classmates rather than getting to know new people – this could be a personality attribute, or it could be connected to working with new people at the same (higher) level as themselves. Working with others at the same higher level may mean that they are no longer the best in the group, and as a result will mean that they suddenly have to make more of an effort; they might feel less secure as a result. My studies have found that the least proficient benefit less from a proficiency-based approach, and often struggle to identify an obvious leader. As such, it is advisable when selecting the learners for each group to ensure that even the lowest-proficiency group contains those who are a step up from the others, but not by too much.

Practical applications

If you teach any L1 lessons, try out Storyline there before you work with it in English. This gives the learners a chance to get used to how it works before they do it in English. You can then begin with something smaller in scale in L2, perhaps based on the topic and language of a chapter or chapters in your coursebook. It is also important to stress that your learners should already be used to working in groups. Note that not every member of the class has to have their own character – it might be that a group is responsible for one character, or that the class together develop the story, as they did with *Fantastic Mr Fox*.

The following is an outline of what a Storyline based on Marcus Pfister's The Rainbow Fish (2007) might look like for elementary learners. This was originally written in German and has been translated into many languages, including English; there are also bilingual versions. It tells the story of a multicoloured fish with shining scales, who considers himself too beautiful to play with the other fish. When another fish asks for one of his scales, the Rainbow Fish refuses, and all the other fish leave him on his own. Feeling lonely, the Rainbow Fish seeks advice from the wise octopus, who suggests that he give his scales to the other fish in order to win them over.

Storyline: The Rainbow Fish

Time:	7 lessons x 45 minutes
Age:	8–9
Key language:	Nouns (*rainbow, fish, sea, octopus, scale*); adjectives (*happy, beautiful*); verbs (*laugh, swim*); simple present, including negative and question forms; modal verbs; stating reasons using *because*
Preparation:	Prepare sheets of paper that can represent the sea. Place these on a frieze or on the walls of the classroom. If you teach art lessons, let the children paint an empty canvas of the sea and display this on the wall. Tell the class that it is empty now because they are going to be working with it and those who live in it in their Storyline. Then prepare a copy of the Rainbow Fish character from the book, a drawing of a little blue fish, and an image of an

octopus, all of which will be placed on the frieze as the story develops. Finally, print out an outline of a fish from the internet for use in Key Question 1, stage 2.

Decide which children will work together. They should sit in these groups at the start of every lesson.

Procedure:

Lesson 1

1. Write Key Question 1 on the board: Which creatures live in the sea?
2. In groups, the children brainstorm what they know in English or in their L1. Write their suggestions on the board.
3. Ask each child to create their own fish character based on this list. They can draw this or use the outline you have prepared.
4. Show them how to attach their drawing to a lollipop stick. To end the lesson, draw an outline of a fish on the whiteboard and ask the children if they know the words for the different parts of the fish. The word you particularly want them to name is *scale* because this is central to the story. The children should put their drawings somewhere safe until the next lesson.

Lesson 2

1. Ask the children to take out their fish from the last lesson. Ask them if they remember the names for the parts of the fish's body.
2. Write on the board:

   My name is

   I have

   I am

   I eat

   Every day I

The children write five facts about their character on a piece of paper, using the sentence starters above. In the last ten minutes, using their lollipop character, they practise introducing themselves to their groupmates.

Lesson 3

1. Before the lesson, put your picture of the Rainbow Fish on the painted canvas, at some distance from where the other fish are going to be placed.
2. Start the lesson by having the children mingle with music playing, holding their fish characters on the lollipop sticks in front of them.

When you stop the music, they should introduce themselves, as their fish characters, to the nearest person. Repeat this several times.

3. The children then place their fish characters still attached to the lollipop sticks, with the descriptive text, on the frieze.
4. Gather the class at the canvas. Ask them if they notice anything that was not there in the last lesson. What can the children tell you about the fish (i.e. the Rainbow Fish) on the canvas? Write their ideas on the board.
5. Write Key Question 2 on the board: Who is the new fish?
6. Read aloud: *The Rainbow Fish was the most beautiful fish in the sea. But he never played with the other fish. I'm too beautiful, he thought.*
7. To round off the lesson, place your picture of the little blue fish close to the Rainbow Fish and ask the children to suggest what might happen next and why. They do this in their groups; tell them you will come back to it next time.

Lesson 4

1. Point at the blue fish on the canvas and ask the class what they think happens next. Their answers will show you how well they understood the first two sentences of the book which you read last time. Someone might use the word 'beautiful'.
2. Read aloud the text where the fish asks for one of the scales, the Rainbow Fish refuses and all the other fish swim away.
3. First, let the learners talk in their groups about what has just happened in the story. Let them tell you what they understand, perhaps using L1 for support; where this is the case, write the L2 words on the board.
4. Draw an outline on the board of the Rainbow Fish and the blue fish. Ask:
   - 'How do you think the little blue fish feels?' Write their suggestions in the form of adjectives around the outline.
   - 'How do you think the Rainbow Fish feels?' Write their suggestions in the form of adjectives around the outline.
5. Each group writes a thought bubble for either the blue fish or Rainbow Fish. (You decide who does what, so the number is even.) They write a whole sentence, which should include one of the words from the board. It might be that some write short sentences such as 'I feel sad', while others attempt longer sentences: 'I feel sad because the Rainbow Fish doesn't want to play'. Either let the groups decide how much to write,

or tell them you want them to give a reason for the feeling. They cut the sentences out and stick them on the canvas.

6. Ask the children to choose five of the words and make their own sentences about themselves to write in their notebooks. This will allow you to see how they have individually understood the meaning of the words and whether they are able to use them. Example: 'I am sad when no one wants to play'; 'I am happy when I play with my friends'. This can be completed for homework.

Lesson 5

1. Ask the children to think on their own about what the Rainbow Fish does next and then to tell their groupmates using L1 or L2. Now read the text where the starfish tells the Rainbow Fish to ask the octopus for advice. How does this compare with their ideas? Do they know what an octopus is? Place the image next to the Rainbow Fish.
2. Write Key Question 3 on the board: <u>What does the octopus tell the Rainbow Fish?</u> Ask the children what they think the octopus says to the Rainbow Fish.
3. Each group writes a sentence. Tell them that they are going to listen to each other's sentences and think about whether the advice was the same. The focus here is on the message rather than the words used.
4. Read the text in which the octopus advises the Rainbow Fish to give away his scales and he says he cannot do it.
5. Play bingo with the target words. Once you have done this, ask each child to choose two of the words they have not used before and write two sentences in their notebook, this time about the story rather than about themselves.

Lesson 6

1. Write Key Question 4 on the board: <u>How do you think the story ends?</u> Before you get to the end of the story, ask the children if they can tell you what the story is about and what has happened so far. If you can, gather them by the frieze and let them point to the things on it.
2. Tell the groups that they are now going to decide how the story ends and show this as a drama. Everyone should have a role, and every role should have at least one line of dialogue. Preparing this will take at least to the end of the lesson.

Lesson 7

1. Warm up with a round of true/false statements. Examples: 'The Rainbow Fish has many colourful scales; he does not want to play with the others; the Rainbow Fish goes to the whale for advice.'
2. Give the children some time to rehearse their role plays.
3. As they watch and listen to each other's role plays, ask them to consider what was common to all the role plays, and what was different; they talk about this with their groupmates.
4. Ask each group for some feedback, and if they can, everybody should try to say one thing.
5. Now place the blue fish close to the Rainbow Fish on the frieze again and read the part of the text where he asks again for a scale and gets one.
6. Ask the children if their fish would also like a scale. Do they think the Rainbow Fish will give them one? Let them move their fish closer to the Rainbow Fish.
7. Read the last part of the text but stop at the point where there is only one scale left. Ask them: How do you think the Rainbow Fish feels now? Why? Each person writes this in their notebook, then compares their sentence or word with what their groupmates have written. Encourage them to use the word 'because' and to state a reason. Did they agree with each other? The group and class discussion may have to be left to the next lesson when you will also read the final part of the book.

Extension:

There are a number of ways you can extend this scheme of work. One leads directly on from the last page in the book. You could ask your learners: Is it right for the other fish to ask for the Rainbow Fish's scales? Is he wrong to say he does not want to give away his scales? Ask them to think about their own possessions. Would they be happy to give something away to someone else who asked for it? In the younger years, this will be in L1, but to link it to L2. Another extension area is a consideration of what it means to be a good friend. Using an outline of a human figure, the children might write the qualities of what a good friend is and does.

You will also have noticed that in my Storyline the children have not read the text themselves, they have listened to the teacher reading. But if you want to bring in reading, use the jigsaw technique: give pairs of learners pieces of text and ask them to arrange the pieces in the correct sequence.

For another task, copy the pictures and text pieces and ask the children to match a picture with an appropriate part of the text. A third suggestion is to give them the L1 translations for the key vocabulary and ask them to find the words in the text.

In Appendix 2, you will find a Storyline template. I use these in my own planning, based on Key Questions rather than lessons, to give an overview of the story, the tasks, the interaction patterns (to make sure there is enough individual work as well as group work), vocabulary/grammar and syllabus links. Columns for 'Time' and 'Materials' are also useful.

Professional development

Questions for reflection

- What do you see as the relative benefits and challenges of making a Storyline from scratch versus using an existing story?
- Consider the mix of proficiencies you are working with at the moment. How could you group the learners for a Storyline project to allow all the children to make a valuable contribution?

Things to try

- Look at the material in your coursebook. Identify a scenario that would lend itself to a story setting and characters that would let you work with the language structures and vocabulary in a chapter or chapters. Use the blank template in Appendix 2 and create an outline.
- Choose a children's book that you think could work well as a Storyline. This could be a book that the children are already familiar with in L1 and are now going to explore in English using Storyline. Think about how the book is structured. What could the Key Questions be? For each Key Question, think of three or four tasks which practise different language skills, grammar or vocabulary.

Further reading

Ahlquist, S. (2013). *Storyline – developing communicative competence in English*. Lund: Studentlitteratur

Ahlquist, S. (2021). *Integrating children's fiction and Storyline in the second language classroom. Education Inquiry 14*(1): pp 105–124.

Final words

I would like to end this book with the words of one young learner in my Storyline study of neighbours in an English town. The children used notebooks to write about the activities they had enjoyed most and those they had enjoyed less. They also used them to record what they had learnt during each week. At the end of the five-week period, they completed a questionnaire. This 12-year-old pupil wrote in L1: 'With Storyline, you never know what is coming next. We did lots of things and most of them were interesting and fun. So, you put more in, and you get more out. I learnt a lot along the way.'

Although this child is referring specifically to the Storyline project, I think that the points he makes also apply more broadly to working with stories. There is the uncertainty about how a story will unfold; the reader becomes absorbed in the environment, the people and the events as they work with tasks that help them improve their English. I hope that you as a teacher have found this book useful, and I wish you and your classes a lot of fun along the way as you explore the wonderful world of stories together.

Appendix 1

Dictogloss (Chapter 4)

_____ wolf looked _____ surprise at _____ blanket,
and _____ out again _____ the pigs.
_____ was shivering, _____ teeth were _____,
he wanted _____ build a _____ with twigs.
_____ banged again _____ the pigs’ _____,
and said _____ his loudest _____,
‘Let me _____ or I’ll _____ your house_____.
It’s up _____ you. It’s _____ choice!’

The _____ looked in _____ at the _____,
and called _____ again to _____ pigs.
He _____ shivering, his _____ were chattering,
_____ wanted to _____ a fire _____ twigs.
He _____ again on _____ pigs’ door,
_____ said in _____ loudest voice,
‘_____ me in _____ I’ll blow _____ house down,
_____ up to _____. It’s your _____!’

The wolf _____ in surprise _____ the blanket,
_____ called out _____ to the _____.
He was _____, his teeth _____chattering,
he _____to build _____ fire with _____.
He banged _____on the _____door,
and _____in his _____voice,
`Let _____ in or _____ blow your _____ down,
It’s _____ to you. _____ your choice!’

Appendix 2

Overview of Storyline content

Key Question	Tasks	Syllabus	Grammar/ Vocabulary	Individual, pair or group	Time	Products for frieze	Materials
1.							
2.							

Bibliography

Ahlquist, S. (2013). *Storyline: Developing communicative competence in the second language learning classroom*. Lund: Studentlitteratur.

Ahlquist, S. (2020). Embedding language-development tasks in lessons based on the magic finger in the primary classroom. *Children's Literature in Language Education (CLELE)*, *8*(2): 64–85.

Ahlquist, S. (2021). Integrating children's fiction and Storyline in the second language classroom. *Education Inquiry*, *14*(1): 105–124.

Anderson, A. (2018). *Neither*. Boston, MA: Little, Brown.

Andrae, G. (1999). *Giraffes can't dance.* London: Orchard Books.

Anholt, L. (2002a). *Cinderboy*. London: Orchard Books.

Anhot, L. (2002b). *Snow White and the seven aliens.* London: Orchard Books.

Armitage, R. & Armitage, D. (2022). *The lighthouse keeper's lunch (45th anniversary edition).* Jefferson City, MO: Scholastic.

Bader, B. (1976). *American picturebooks from Noah's Ark to The Beast Within*. New York: Macmillan.

Barroux, S. (2016). *Welcome*. New York: Little Bee Books.

Bell, S. & Harkness, S. (2006). *Storyline – Promoting language across the curriculum*. Royston: The United Kingdom Literacy Association (UKLA).

Bladon, R. (2018). *Anne Frank*. Oxford: Oxford Bookworms.

Bland, J. (Ed.) (2015). *Teaching English to young learners: Critical issues in language teaching with 3–12-year-olds*. London: Bloomsbury.

Bland, J. (Ed.) (2018). *Using literature in English language education: Challenging reading for 8–18-year-olds.* London: Bloomsbury.

Bland, J. (2023). *Compelling stories for English language learners: Creativity, interculturality and critical literacy.* London: Bloomsbury.

Bland, J. & Lütge, C. (Eds.) (2013). *Children's literature in second language education*. London: Bloomsbury.

Brenna, B. (2013). How graphic novels support reading comprehension strategy development in children. In *Literacy*, *47*(2): 88–94.

Briggs, R. (1995). *The Snowman*. Oxford: Oxford University Press.

Briggs, R. (1980). Gentleman Jim. London: Jonathan Cape.

Briggs, R. (1982). When the wind blows. London: Jonathan Cape.

Briggs, R. (1998). Ethel and Ernest. London: Jonathan Cape.

Brinkmann, S. (2015). Alex Rider – Stormbreaker: A Graphic Novel Experience. *Children's Literature in Language Education (CLELE)*, 3(2): 61–84.

Browne, A. (1992). *Zoo*. London: Random House Publishing.

Brunsmeier, S. & Kolb, A. (2017). 'Picturebooks go digital – The potential of story apps for the primary EFL classroom'. *Children's Literature in Language Education (CLELE)*, *5*(1): 1–20.

Burrows, P. & Foster, M. (2007). *Escape* (Oxford Bookworms Starters). Oxford: Oxford University Press.

Cabrera, M. P. & Martinez, P. B. (2001). The effects of repetition, comprehension checks and gestures on primary school children in an EFL situation. *ELT Journal*, *55*: 281–288.

Calzada, A. & García Mayo, M. P. (2020). Child EFL learners' attitudes towards a collaborative writing task: An exploratory study. *Language Teaching for Young Learners*, *2*(1): 52–72.

Cameron, L. (2001). *Teaching languages to young learners*. Cambridge: Cambridge University Press.

Cole, B. (1997). *Princess Smartypants*. London: Puffin.

Cole, B. (2017). *Princess Smartypants and the fairy geek mother*. London: Hodder Children's Books.

Common European Framework of Reference for Languages. (2001), updated version 2022. https://www.coe.int/en/web/common-european-framework-reference-languages.

Dahl, R. (2016). *The magic finger,* colour edition. London: Puffin.

Dahl, R. (2016). *Fantastic Mr Fox*, colour edition. London: Puffin.

Dahl, R. (2009). *Revolting rhymes*. New York: Viking Penguin.

De Fabris, B.K. (2014). *The summaries of 150 classic fairy tales*. Scotts Valley, CA: Createspace Independent Publishing Platform.

Delisle, G. (2006). *Pyongyang*. London: Jonathan Cape Publishers.

Dutke, S. & Rinck, M. (2006). Multimedia learning: Working memory and the learning of word and picture diagrams. In *Learning and Instruction*, *16*: 526–537. Education, CLELE.

Ellis, G. & Brewster, J., 2014. *Tell it again! The storytelling handbook for primary English language teachers*. London: British Council, www.teachingenglish.org.uk.

Elsner, D. & Viebrock, B. (2013). Developing multiliteracies in the 21st century: Motives for new approaches of teaching and learning foreign languages. In Part 1 of D. Elsner, S. Helff, & B. Viebrock (Eds.). *Films, graphic novels & visuals: Developing multiliteracies in foreign language education – an interdisciplinary approach*. Munster, Germany: LIT Verlag: 17–32.

Enever, J. (Ed.) (2011). Early language learning in Europe (ELLiE). London: British Council. Available at https://www.teachingenglish.org.uk/article/ellie-early-language-learning-europe. Last accessed on 15 September 2022.)

Escott, J. (2000). *Dead man's island*. Oxford: Oxford University Press.

Fordham, F. (2018). *To kill a mockingbird* (graphic novel). Portsmouth, New Hampshire: Heinemann.

Fordham, F. (2022) *Brave new world* (graphic novel). New York: Vintage Publishing.

Gaiman, N. (2002). *Coraline*. New York: Harper Collins.

Gaiman, N. & Russell, C. P. (2008). *Coraline*. New York: Harper Trophy.

Garcia Bermejo, M. L. & Fleta Guillén, M. T. (2013). The 'art' of teaching creative story writing. Chapter 18 in J. Bland, & C. Lütge, (Eds.), *Children's literature in second language education*. London: Bloomsbury.

Garland, S. (2012). *Azzi in between*. London: Frances Lincoln Children's Books.

Gray, J. (2016). ELT materials: Claims, critiques and controversies. In G. Hall (ed.), *The Routledge handbook of English language teaching*. Abingdon: Routledge, 95–108.

Ghosn, I. K. (2013). *Storybridge to second language literacy: The theory, research and practice of teaching English with children's literature.* Charlotte, N.C: Information Age Publishing.

Grant, M. (2014). *Gone*. New York: Harper Collins.

Hall, G. (2016). Using literature in ELT. Chapter 32 in G. Hall (ed.). *The Routledge handbook of English language teaching*. Abingdon, Oxon: Routledge.

Hasselgreen, A., Drew, I, & Sörheim, B. (2012). *The young language learner: Research-based insights into teaching and learning*. Bergen: Fagbokförlaget.

Horowitz, A. (2006). *Stormbreaker*. London: Puffin Books.

Horwitz, E. K. (2010). 'Research timeline. Foreign and second language anxiety'. *Language Teaching*, *43*:154–167.

Huh, S. & Suh, Y.M. (2015). Becoming critical readers of graphic novels: Bringing graphic novels into Korean elementary literacy lessons. In *English Teaching*, *70*(1): 123–149.

Hutchins, P. (1968). *Rosie's walk*. New Jersey: Prentice Hall.

Ibrahim, N. (2020). The multilingual picturebook in English language teaching: Linguistic and cultural identity. *Children's Literature in English Language Education (CLELE)*, *8*(2): 12–38.

Jaffe, M. & Hurwich, T. (2019). *Worth a thousand words: Using graphic novels to teach visual and verbal literacy.* San Francisco, CA: Jossey-Bass.

Kaminski, A. (2013). From reading pictures to understanding a story in the foreign language. *Children's Literature in Language Education (CLELE)*, *1*(1): 19–38.

Kinney, J. (2008). Diary of a wimpy kid. New York: Puffin.

Koushki Larkin, A. (2019). Engaging English learners through literature, fairy tales, and drama. *International Journal of Applied Linguistics & English Literature*, *8*(2): 138–144.

Krashen, S. D. (1982). *Principles and practice in second language acquisition*. Oxford: Pergamon Press.

Krashen, S. D. (2004). *The power of reading: insights from the research* (2nd edition). Westport, CT: Libraries Unlimited.

Krashen, S. & Bland, J. (2014). Compelling comprehensible input, Academic language and school libraries. *Children's Literature in Language Education (CLELE)* *2*(2): 1–12

Lamb, M. (2017). The motivational dimension of language teaching. *Language Teaching* *50*(3): 301–346.

Laufer, B. & Aviad-Levitzky, T. (2017). 'What Type of Vocabulary Knowledge Predicts Reading Comprehension: Word Meaning Recall or Word Meaning Recognition?' *The Modern Language Journal* *104*(4): 729–741. Hoboken: Wiley Online.

Lichtman, K. & VanPatten, W. (2021) – Was Krashen right? Forty years later. *Foreign Language Annals* 54 (2); Wiley Online.

Lofthouse, L. (2007). *Ziba came on a boat*. Melbourne, Australia: Puffin.

Long, M. (2020). Optimal input for language learning: Genuine, simplified, elaborated or modified elaborated? *Language Teaching* *53*(2): 169–182.

Love, J. (2018). *Julian is a mermaid*. Somerville, MA: Candlewick Press.

Macaro, E. & Mutton, T. (2009). Developing reading achievement in primary learners of French: inferencing strategies versus exposure to 'graded readers'. *Language Learning Journal*, *37*(2): 165–182.

Matteuzzi, F. & Maraggi, M. (2022). *Banksy*. London: Prestel.

Mayer, R. E. (2021). *Multimedia learning*, 3rd edition. Cambridge: Cambridge University Press.

McCloud, S. (1993). *Understanding comics: The invisible art.* New York: Harper Collins.

McGoon, G. (2015). *The royal heart*. Claremont, CA: Pelekinesis Press.

Mombian.com: The Mombian Database of LGBTQ Family Books. https://mombian.com/database/

Morpurgo, M. (1982). *Warhorse*. London: Kaye and Ward.

Morpurgo, M. (1996). *The butterfly lion*. New York: HarperCollins.

Morpurgo, M. (2003). *Private Peaceful*. New York: HarperCollins.

Morpurgo, M. (2007). *Singing for Mrs Pettigrew: A storymaker's journey*. London: Walker Books Ltd.

Morpurgo, M. (2009). *Running wild.* New York: HarperCollins.

Morpurgo, M. (2014). *Orchard's book of Aesop's fables*. London: Orchard.

Mourao, S. (2014). *Picturebook: Object of discovery.* Chapter 7 in J. Bland, & C. Lutge (Eds.), Children's literature in second language education, 71–82.

Mourao, S. (2016). Picturebooks in the primary EFL classroom: Authentic literature for an authentic response. *Children's Literature in English Language Education (CLELE)*, *4*(1): 25–43.

Nation, P. (2007). The four strands. *Innovation in language learning and teaching 1*(1): 1–12.

Nikolov, M. & Timpe-Laughlin, V. (2021). Assessing young learners' foreign language abilities. *Language Teaching 54*(1): 1–37.

Nordlund, M. (2016). EFL textbooks for young learners: A comparative analysis of vocabulary. *Education Inquiry 7*(1): 47–68.

Nordlund, M. & Norberg, C. (2020). Vocabulary in EFL teaching materials for young learners. *International Journal of Language Studies 14*(1): 89–116. Ipswich, MA: EBSCO Publishing.

Nosy Crow & Bryan, E. (2015). *Jack and the Beanstalk*. London: Nosy Crow.

Olearski, J. (2010). *Mr Football.* Innsbruck: Helbling.

PEPELT. Picturebooks in European primary English language teaching. Available at: https://pepelt21.com/

Pfister, M. (2007). *The rainbow fish*. New York: NorthSouth Books.

Pike, O. (2020). *Prince Henry*, 4th revised edition. London: Pop'n'Olly.

Pike, O. (2018). *The prince and the frog*. London: Jessica Kingsley Publishers.

Pinter, A. (2007). Benefits of peer–peer interaction: 10-year-old children practicing with a communication task. *Language Teaching Research 11*: 189–207.

Pinter, A. (2017). *Teaching young language learners*, 2nd edition. Oxford: Oxford University Press.

Poston, A. (2020). *The princess and the fangirl: A Geekarella fairy tale*. Philadelphia, PA: Quirk Books.

Qiang, W., Zehang, C. & Xianglin, X. (2020). Improving Chines students' English reading through graded readers: Rationale, strategies and effectiveness. *Language Teaching for Young Learners 2*,(2): 262-301

Rabley, S. (2008). *Dino's day in London*: London: Penguin.

Radari, G. (2022). *Telling stories wrong.* New York: Enchanted Lion Books.

Raynham, A. (2018). *Stephen Hawking*. Oxford: Oxford Bookworms.

Raynham, A. (2019). *Usain Bolt*. Oxford: Oxford Bookworms.

Read, C. (2007). *500 Activities for the Primary Classroom.* Oxford: Macmillan.

Satrapi, M. (2003). *Persepolis*. New York: Pantheon Books.

Schmidt, R. (2010). Attention, awareness, and individual differences in language learning. In W. M. Chan, S. Chi, K. N. Cin, J. Istanto, M. Nagami, J. W. Sew, T. Suthiwan, & I. Walker, *Proceedings of CLaSIC 2010*, Singapore. Singapore: National University of Singapore: 721–737.

Scieska, J. 1991). *The True Story of the Three Little Pigs.* London: Puffin Books.

Simon, M. (2022). The benefits of using fairy tales in EFL classrooms. *Asian Education Studies*, *7*(3): 1-7.

shereads (2023). Young adult (book list). https://shereads.com/category/book-lists/ya/

Tan, S. (2007). *The Arrival*. London: Hodder Education.

Teller, D. (2019). *All the ever afters: The untold story of Cinderella's stepmother*. New York: William Morrow Paperbacks.

Trivizas, E. (1997). *The three little wolves and the big bad pig.* New York: Margaret K. McElderberry Books.

Twain, M. (2011). *The prince and the pauper*. London: HarperCollins.

Umansky, K. (2015). *Prince Frog Face*. Edinburgh: Barrington Stoke.

United Nations. *The 17 goals*. Available at: https://sdgs.un.org/goals

Vicary, T. (2007). *Death in the freezer*. Oxford: Oxford University Press.

Vygotsky, L. (1978). *Mind in society.* Cambridge: Harvard University Press.

Wajnryb, R. (1990). *Grammar dictation*. Oxford: Oxford University Press.

Wallner, L. (2019). Gutter talk: Co-constructing narratives using comics in the classroom. *Scandinavian Journal of Educational Research*, *63*(6): 819–838.

Wang, Q., Chen, Z., & Qi, X. (2020). Improving Chinese students' English reading through graded readers: Rationale, strategies and effectiveness. *Language Teaching for Young Learners* *2*(2): 262–301.

Waring, R. (2000). The Oxford University Press Guide to the Why and How of Using Graded Readers. Tokyo: Oxford University Press.

Waring, R., & Takaki, M. (2003). At what rate do learners learn and retain new vocabulary from a graded reader? *Reading in a Foreign language 15*(2): 130–163.

Watkins, P. (2018). Extensive reading for Primary ELT. Cambridge Papers in ELT Series. Cambridge: Cambridge University Press. Available at: https://www.cambridge.org/us/files/7915/7488/5311/CambridgePapersInELT_ExtReadingPrimary_2018_ONLINE.pdf.

Webb. S. & Nation, P. (2017). *How vocabulary is learned.* Oxford: Oxford University Press.

Williams, G. & Normann, A. [eds]. (2021). *Literature for the English Classroom: Theory into Practice, 2nd edition*. Fagbotforlaget.

Wilson, J. (2007). *Kiss*. New York: Doubleday.

Wilson, J. (2008). *Best friends*. New York: Yearling.

Wilson, J. (2012). *Four children and it*. London: Puffin.

Wilson, J. (2021). *The Primrose Railway Children*. London: Puffin.

Wodinsky, M., & Nation, P. (1988). Learning from graded readers. *Reading in a Foreign Language 5*(1): 155–161.

Wright, A. (1997). *Creating stories with children*. Oxford: Oxford University Press.

Wright, A. (2013). Stories as symphonies. Chapter 19 in J. Bland, & C. Lütge (Eds). *Children's literature in second language education*. London: Bloomsbury.